Letting Go and Living On

Mark Lea

3P
PUBLISHING

First published in 2020 in the UK

3P Publishing
C E C, London Road
Corby
NN17 5EU

A catalogue number for this book is available from the British Library

ISBN: 978-1-9163940-9-4

Cover design: Marie-Louise O'Neill

This book is dedicated to my soulmate, Julie and all our family and friends who have given incredible support - thank you.

Contents Page

Chapter 1

The End

The digital clock above the bed showed 8.43pm at the devastating, heart-breaking time when Julie Marie Lea took her final breath. The date was Thursday, June 20, 2019. Coincidentally, my soulmate had died on my 45th birthday. I was holding her left hand gently and stroking her. One last kiss on her forehead to say goodbye.

On the other side of the bed was her older brother David. He had been sitting loyally next to Julie almost entirely for those 36 hours when she was finally out of pain at St Michael's Hospice, Basingstoke. He didn't want to let her go. None of us did.

We both looked up at the clock at the same time. We knew what had happened. There were no words. It was all over. So suddenly.

Julie's parents John and Linda Fisher were also in the room, along with David's partner Eileen. The family had arrived in Hampshire the previous morning and we knew this tragic moment was going to happen pretty quickly. The final leg of this journey was always going to be a matter of hours or days – certainly not weeks or months.

The reality had hit me on the previous Monday evening during a private chat with a psychologist at Basingstoke and North Hampshire Hospital. There was nothing more that could be done to save Julie's life. She would not be coming back home. I knew she wouldn't make it until the weekend. Maybe she wanted to wait for my birthday and say farewell.

We had only been down there for a couple of weeks. At this stage, initially she was supposed to be starting the long road to recovery from major surgery to remove an appendix tumour, but she was never given time to fight against it. There was no chance of winning this battle between life and death.

'It's not fair!'

Several times, sitting in her hospital bed and feeling the unbearable pain, she would make that declaration.

'Mark, I've got cancer.'

What's the answer? There was nothing to say, really.

'I know.'

Occasionally I would add 'Sorry', because there was nothing that anybody could do now. Everyone had done their best and sometimes that's not simply good enough.

Julie was given the best opportunity thanks to top-class care. Ultimately, though, it was only a very short battle against cancer. That doesn't make it easier or fairer. She could have been fighting for years; instead, it was only a few weeks. She didn't even celebrate her 40th birthday. The special day was nearly eight months away. That's certainly not fair. It wouldn't have surprised Julie's family and friends to learn that she was already making plans and starting the countdown to her birthday. Of course, inevitably, there was also a list to go with it, neatly written in purple and green ink. Tragically, due to illness, she never even reached the second half of those ideas and suggestions.

1. Read a Harry Potter book
2. Watch a James Bond film
3. Properly run a 10k
4. Join a new club
5. Watch a new boxset
6. Learn how to do a roundhouse kick
7. Watch the sunset on a beach
8. Volunteer for a charity
9. Host a 90s party
10. Write a book of poems
11. Watch one *Star Wars* film
12. Watch *The Shawshank Redemption*
13. Skydive or wing walk
14. Learn to play a new instrument
15. Learn a new sport
16. Watch *Brassed Off*

40 before 40!

At the end of the list was an extra special bonus: 41 – meet Gary Barlow! Julie wrote six short poems and only started to plan ticking off some of those items on the list. On her final afternoon, she was told that I had somehow agreed to do a skydive with Julie's close friend Alex in aid of charity. It was one of the last conversations that she would have heard.

Following a series of messages, Alex and I had arranged to talk at 8pm. The missed calls came when, worryingly, Julie's breathing patterns began to change. I pressed the emergency alarm in her room to get medical help. Immediately, the nurses knew what was coming. Again, it happened very quickly and the pain was over.

Only a few hours earlier, we had thankfully shared some time together while the rest of the family took a well-earned break from the bedside. There is some small consolation in knowing that Julie heard me reading out all the heartfelt messages from her wonderful group of friends, which had been collected on my phone over a couple of days.

Over the weekend, it became clear that Julie's health was declining rapidly. I saw it first-hand, but everyone else must have realised that something was terribly wrong when she stopped replying to messages on her phone. It was highly unusual for her.

Just before we left home together for the final time, Julie had set up a small group of 'favourites' on my phone with instructions for those friends to receive full updates on what would have been major surgery and a spell in the intensive care unit. There was also a private group on Facebook where she had chosen who would find out first what was happening. Julie's page is still being updated with tributes. So, there was absolutely no doubt in my mind over what needed to be done immediately after the hospice staff had cleaned Julie's body and put her in clean pyjamas for the chapel of rest. Briefly, I went inside to see her for the last time and, after probably 15 seconds, I needed to step away. It was too much emotionally for me.

It was around 10.30pm when I moved slowly and privately into a family lounge at the hospice to start making those phone calls to Julie's friends and my family. What can you say? It's all over and we're all hurting so much, because, as she said, it's not fair.

David made the call to Chambers & Brighty funeral directors in Wellingborough. We went back to our accommodation overnight and gathered again the next morning for a discussion that none of us could have expected. Burial or cremation – what would Julie want? We never had the conversation; why would we, when she was only in her thirties? We agreed on cremation and returned to the hospice. The family set off home and I made an appointment to get Julie's death certificate that morning, because I certainly didn't want to return to Basingstoke early next week. When I left the town around noon, I was alone and immediately I knew that I would need lots of support

Chapter 2

Hospital

A text message flashed on my phone mid-afternoon on Tuesday, April 9, 2019.

Julie explained that she had collapsed at work just after lunchtime and an ambulance was called to North Kesteven District Council's offices in Sleaford.

At the same time, my grandma was being treated at Pilgrim Hospital, Boston, and I needed to visit her. So I quickly left the *Lincolnshire Free Press* office in Spalding and made a decision to head down the A16 before going to check on Julie.

It turned out to be the right thing to do, because Julie was still waiting in the Accident and Emergency Department at Lincoln County Hospital when I arrived. Several hours later, she was finally seen by a doctor and put in a private bay. After midnight, I went home because she was comfortable.

The previous night, Julie had felt a lump around her stomach and she had planned to make a doctor's appointment. It turned out to be a mass in the right lower abdomen. This is how it all started – the first time she had been physically ill enough to go into hospital. Julie's concerns understandably grew, because her favourite Auntie Beryl had died from ovarian cancer.

Over the next couple of months, she had three spells in Lincoln County Hospital and another couple of days in Kettering General Hospital in Northamptonshire on a bank holiday weekend with her family. But the doctors were struggling to contain the infection and Julie was very poorly even on those days when she was out of hospital. At home, she moved into the spare room to get more comfortable but often she struggled to get up and down the stairs. There were several 999 calls when the pain became too much to bear.

At first, they were talking about a collection or mass – possibly fluid that could be drained. But the infection wasn't clearing up, despite the strongest antibiotics. Julie's inflammatory markers were quite high and she was unable to have a colonoscopy. There was so much frustration, plus many moments of boredom in hospital waiting for another test or any update.

There were a series of blood tests and scans but, ultimately, the case was sent by consultant colorectal surgeon Aarti Varma at Lincoln County Hospital to specialists in Basingstoke. Julie was given an outpatient appointment with consultant surgeon Sanjeev Dayal on Wednesday, May 15.

Julie knew that she didn't want to read any part of the discharge letters from doctors because of her anxiety. Fair enough, I totally understood why, but she had privately checked out on Google what happens at the Peritoneal Malignancy Institute at Basingstoke and North Hampshire Hospital.

So it was probably a bigger shock to me when we were told that the lower abdominal mass was an appendix tumour. The surgical plans for complete tumour removal were explained and we were given more information by clinical specialist nurse Linda Cass.

The medical term for Julie's tumour is pseudomyxoma peritonei, a rare cancer around the appendix. The average operating time for a major peritonectomy is ten hours. Patients usually stay in hospital for three weeks, then recovery at home takes around three months. The mortality risk is 1% to 2%, although we weren't too concerned because of Julie's age and previous medical history. She understood those basic facts and she was prepared for surgery.

Obviously, patients must be as physically fit as possible to help recovery. The recommendation is exercising each day, a good well-balanced diet and supplements. Julie had been losing weight by regularly going to the gym, although she wasn't eating regularly. I could tell that there was clear concern on the faces of any medical professional when Julie told them how much weight had been lost in such a short space of time.

At the end of May, Julie was back in Lincoln County Hospital and they were still struggling to deal with the infection. She was desperate to get out of hospital and on a Friday afternoon, I made calls to Miss Varma and Mrs Cass pleading for more help. Finally, Julie was allowed home but at least we had a date the following week to go back to Basingstoke.

Surgery was planned for Thursday, June 6, and Julie checked into ward C2 on the Tuesday morning.

Nurses recorded her details including blood pressure, pulse, temperature, weight and height. There were blood tests and x-rays, plus ECG and bowel preparation – although Julie's body simply wouldn't take the laxative called Picolax, as it made her horribly sick, just as it had done in Lincoln only a few days earlier.

We met the palliative care team dedicated to people affected by life-threatening illness. One by one over only a few hours, we were introduced to the anaesthetist, physiotherapy team, peritoneal malignancy specialist nurses, pharmacist, nutrition team and stoma care nurses. Julie was also given patient-controlled analgesia to control pain relief via a button, although she was initially reluctant to use it.

Everything appeared to be ready. It seemed like the worst-case scenario would be a more complicated operation and longer recovery period. Late on Wednesday night, I went back to the accommodation for relatives – a single en suite bedroom within a four-bedroom shared flat. Within an hour, Julie called to say the consultant had made another visit and the operation was called off because the calcium levels in the blood had raised concerns about her heart under anaesthetic. Looking back now, I strongly believe they had seen CT scans and realised that surgery could not be done because the cancer cells were too aggressive. I understand why we wouldn't have been told that at the time, though.

A few days later, the consultant said chemotherapy was not guaranteed either, because this was an aggressive peritoneal tumour. Another massive blow and still no results from a biopsy. No updates at all over several days. Questions needed to be asked.

Julie told the consultant three times, 'I'm going to die, aren't I?' with different responses after the diagnosis, surgery cancellation and chemotherapy being ruled out as well. At first, it was a firm 'No,' and then the reply became 'We'll do our best.'

Being together 24/7 in hospital was the toughest time and nobody else knows exactly what happened. There was also a lot of information to digest and pass on for family and friends. Julie couldn't get comfortable in hospital. She was constantly in pain and she asked me to stay overnight with her instead of going back to the accommodation. The staff were happy to provide a camp bed, sheets and pillows. We shared some special times together watching TV and films on my laptop, in between regular visits from the nursing staff.

So much happened and everything changed quickly – but there was no progress.

There was no chance of eating a small meal – Julie couldn't even manage a couple of slices of toast – so total parenteral nutrition was given intravenously into a vein via a central line with several ports allowing more than one infusion. Although it stopped her sickness, Julie absolutely hated the naso-gastric tube through the nose into the stomach. She was delighted when it was removed.

Julie's family visited her each weekend and a couple of friends also came down one evening. She was always trying to put on a brave face for everyone despite all the discomfort. However, I was in the unique situation of knowing the truth and seeing the bravery of fighting pain.

Over the second weekend in Basingstoke, Julie's health clearly declined rapidly and I was given devastating news on the Monday night with another update the next day. She wasn't well enough to travel to a hospice closer to family and friends in Northamptonshire, even though a place had been provisionally booked. At this stage, we were talking about days rather than weeks or months.

Officially, they were planning another CT scan on the Wednesday morning. Privately, I was told this wouldn't happen and the ward matron was very strong with her colleagues in making sure Julie didn't need to go through that again. The cancer was too aggressive and nothing more could be done.

For a couple of days before going into the hospice, she couldn't communicate clearly. At times, there would be a delay in her answer when we assumed she hadn't heard the question. Friends started to contact me directly or I would see names flash up on her phone and explain to them that Julie was too ill to reply.

Although nothing else could be done, I'm completely convinced that Julie was given exceptional care. We met some incredible people.

Doctors and nurses tried their best to control the infection. The specialist team in Basingstoke were amazing but the cancer cells were too aggressive even for some of the best people in the country who did everything to help Julie.

She had wonderful support from the consultants, specialist nurses, dietician, psychiatrist and palliative care team, plus, of course, those at the hospice who finally got Julie comfortable and out of pain.

Obviously, there were a few incidents along the way that perhaps could have gone better – maybe even a couple of 'if only' moments – but generally Julie's treatment was exceptional. Her final night in hospital was a perfect example and I'll never forget what happened.

A special mention here must go to Gemma who was the nurse on duty that night on the far end of C2 ward where Julie's room was next to the entrance doors. What a wonderful young woman, who showed compassion beyond all the professional training; this was about being a beautiful person.

She decided to rearrange the whole room so that Julie's bed would be next to me. If we needed more help, I was told to ask anything. In the middle of the night, when Julie couldn't sleep, Gemma brought in an armchair to make it more comfortable for her sitting up straight. In the morning, we needed to work together just to get Julie to go to the toilet because she couldn't lift herself. Everything was about easing the pain. Gemma wanted us to stay close together and must have known life was coming to an end in front of our eyes. It also meant that Julie and I held hands for most of the night, which was very special.

Her parents, her brother and his partner arrived on the Wednesday morning at a hugely traumatic time when the ambulance staff and nurses were moving Julie from C2 ward to a stretcher for the transfer to St Michael's Hospice. We were only a couple of minutes away from the main hospital building but Julie was badly sick on that journey.

For 36 hours in the hospice, at least Julie was comfortable and out of pain. She would have heard the conversations and the silence. Most importantly, she knew that she was surrounded by the love of her family.

Chapter 3

Funeral

Monday, July 8

The toughest day. Yet it was beautiful. So emotional and what an amazing turnout of family, friends and work colleagues. It shows how much Julie was loved by so many wonderful people.

The Lea family arrived at the Fishers' home in Albert Road, Wellingborough, around an hour before the funeral directors were due to come. Looking at the hearse brought home the reality as the limousine took us to the crematorium. It was nice that Eileen noticed how many people waiting outside were dressed in pink as requested. David and I helped to carry Julie's coffin inside.

I knew the order of service and I thought that I would break down at certain moments. The big one came, as expected, with 'Never Forget' by Take That. My sister Sarah next to me helped and I wanted to stay until the end of the song.

Walking out at the end of the ceremony, I struggled again. There were so many people I didn't really know at first, then came all her friends and colleagues. It was a lovely surprise to see some people when I didn't expect them to come over. It was good to talk to people at the wake as well. I completely broke down again when I got home at the end of such a tough day. I was surrounded my family, for which I was grateful, but at the same time I wanted to be left alone.

IN LOVING MEMORY OF

JULIE MARIE LEA
13th February 1980 - 20th June 2019

Monday 8th July 2019 at 12.00 noon
Nene Valley Crematorium, Wellingborough

Nene Valley Crematorium, Wellingborough
Funeral celebrant: Ruth Stewart
Entrance music: 'Shine' – Take That

Opening words

Today we will celebrate the life of Julie, to give thanks for knowing her and to express gratitude for the days and years shared with her. We are here to remember this unique person and celebrate the life that she lived. By remembering the best of Julie, you will strengthen the memory of her within you and that will never leave. It is hoped that this ceremony will also serve to comfort her family and all of you here today.

An untimely death raises questions for all of us. It is difficult to think that there must somewhere, somehow be some purpose for this. Sometimes there simply are no answers, however hard we look. Julie's death was too early and that is the most difficult for us to understand.

You have come here to respect the life that she lived, to recall the joy and love and friendship that Julie gave to you all and to remember her as she would want you to. You have all been touched by her life, so remember Julie with kindness, with warmth, with fond memories, with love and affection, and above all with gratitude for what knowing her has brought to your life.

Poem: Only We Who Grieve (read by Ruth Stewart)

'Tis only we who grieve
They do not leave
They are not gone
They look upon us still
They walk among the valleys now
They stride upon the hill
Their smile is in the summer sky
Their grace is in the breeze
Their memories whisper in the grass
Their calm is in the trees
Their light is in the winter snow

Their tears are in the rain
Their merriment runs in the brook
Their laughter in the lane
Their gentleness is in the flowers
They sigh in autumn leaves
They do not leave
They are not gone
'Tis only we who grieve

Julie's story

Julie's story began on February 13, 1980, when she was born at Kettering General Hospital to proud parents Linda and John Fisher. Joining older brother David, Julie completed this close and loving family. Julie grew up at Albert Road, Wellingborough, attending Victoria Infants and Juniors before moving onto Wrenn Secondary School. A bright and popular student, Julie enjoyed school – a great favourite of her teachers.

Her strongest talents lay in English, drama and music and, in any school production, from nativity plays through to musicals, she played a part – loving to perform on stage. This interest continued outside of school as well. Her lovely singing voice was put to good use in the All Saints Church choir as she grew up. Having progressed through the Brownies to the Guides, Julie was an active player in the Wellingborough Gang Show and was to become a valued member of the Wellingborough Operatic Society, appearing in several productions, perhaps one of her most memorable performances was as a nun in *The Sound of Music*.

Leaving school at the age of eighteen after A levels, Julie followed her dream and went to Nene College to study media and business studies with the aim of becoming a print journalist. Julie had very tiny, neat handwriting which proved very useful when she was learning Teeline shorthand. She completed her work experience at the *Evening Telegraph* and it was here, in July 1999, that she met Mark. Their friendship turned into more and they were married on June 14, 2003, at Wellingborough Register Office.

After successfully finishing her course, Julie secured her first job at the *Herald & Post* in Northampton. Beginning as a news reporter, Julie was good at her job and promotions followed until she reached the position of sub-editor. She also worked in the Bedford office before choosing to leave the *Herald & Post* and move to the *Cambridge News* in a different role, designing templates for a new editorial system. She worked alongside Mark on the news desk for some of this time. Julie then found herself at a crossroads in her career and she decided to leave the world of newsprint and to move into a communications role with the City of Lincoln Council. Mark also found work in Lincolnshire so he and Julie set up home in Sleaford.

Julie's confidence was boosted when she was approached to join North Kesteven District Council in Sleaford to work in their communications team. Involved in designing and producing the monthly newsletter, writing press releases and looking after the council's social media outlets, Julie loved the job, enjoying working with her colleagues in the team and the increased responsibility. Elections saw her working throughout the night to monitor the counting of the votes and any communications required at such a tense and pressured event. The job was a good move for Julie and her proud family watched this talented woman blossom into the role.

When the children were young, the Fishers spent many of their holidays on the east coast. They did visit the Lake District, Wales and Devon but the east coast held their hearts. Julie loved walking on the beach and especially loved the coastal walk from Hemsby to Winterton-on-Sea. Later on with Mark, she was to visit Paris and, with her friends, the beautiful city of Madrid and the island of

Cyprus. Julie and Mark would often combine work with pleasure by spending a weekend away when he would be covering a football game. Encouraged by her dad, Julie had long had an interest in football and enjoyed supporting Rushden & Diamonds while Mark was reporting on their games. She also supported Tottenham Hotspur, but a soft spot for Teddy Sheringham and his team-mates may have been the reason for that.

Julie was very close to her parents, especially her dad, and she would often come back to Wellingborough for the weekend when she and her dad would take long walks together. With a brilliant sense of humour, Julie was a loving and caring person who thought of others first. She was a very determined lady and completed the Race for Life twice and had her head shaved to raise money for cancer charities. Julie and her brother David adored one another – from a distance! As she always said, they got on a lot better over the phone.

A special passion for Julie was music. Pop music to be more precise, Take That to be even closer and Gary Barlow to be exact. She had seen her idols several times and knew their music from back to front. Julie made sure she listened to Radio 1 to keep up to date with contemporary pop, although her music tastes did broaden a little as she got older.

This fun-loving, wonderful woman became ill on April 9. It is hard to imagine the devastation felt by this very close family when the seriousness of her illness was diagnosed. Despite being admitted to a specialist care unit for her rare condition, Julie passed away on June 20, far too soon at the age of only 39.

Julie was a fantastic person, making her way through life with laughter, charm and love. She loved many things in her world – Gary Barlow, Wimpy burgers, working cross-stitch patterns and making Tatty Teddies with great skill from her mum, cats, walking on the beach, rom-coms, *The Big Bang Theory* and *Friends* – every script memorised – but most of all, of course, she loved the people around her – her friends, wonderful family and adored husband Mark.

Julie will never be forgotten and, despite being on this earth for far too short a time, has created with you all many wonderful memories which you can share and treasure forever.

Reflection: 'Long Road to Ruin' – Foo Fighters
Poem: Feel No Guilt in Laughter – author unknown (read by Ruth Stewart)

Feel no guilt in laughter; she'd know how much you care.
Feel no sorrow in a smile that she is not here to share.
You cannot grieve forever; she would not want you to.
She'd hope that you could carry on the way you always do.
So, talk about the good times and the way you showed you cared,
The days you spent together, all the happiness you shared.

Let memories surround you. A word someone may say
Will suddenly recapture a time, an hour, a day,
That brings her back as clearly as though she were still here,
And fills you with the feeling that she is always near.
For if you keep those moments, you will never be apart
And she will live forever locked safely within your heart.

Committal music: Theme tune to *Friends*

Be thankful for the life of Julie. For the love she gave and inspired in others. For the friendships she treasured. For her contribution to your world. Nothing good about Julie's life will be lost because it was of benefit to you. What greater honour, when a person who has touched our lives moves forward, they leave behind in each of us, the best of what they were.

In sorrow but without fear, in love and appreciation, we commit Julie's body to its natural end.

Julie, your strength of character and caring nature, your sense of fun and love for life, we commit to our memories. Your loves and friendships, we commit to our hearts. With sorrow, we bid you farewell. With love, we leave you in peace.

Closing words

I am sure that each of you will remember different stories, different comments, different feelings from your contact with Julie for she has made a huge impact on your world. She was a great inspiration to those she loved and will continue to be so.

Each human life is unique and that is why we grieve. Look through the whole world and there is no one like the one you have lost. But Julie still lives on in your memories and, though no longer a visible part of your lives, she will always remain a member of your family or circle through the influence she has had on you and the special part she has played in your lives. As long as you remember Julie, she will live on.

Poem: When We Lose Someone – author unknown (read by David Fisher)

When we lose someone we love it seems that
time stands still. What moves through us is a silence,
a quiet sadness, a longing for one more day,
one more word, one more touch,
we may not understand why you left this earth so soon,
or why you left before we were ready to say good-bye,
but little by little,
we begin to remember not just that you died,

but that you lived.
And that your life gave us memories too beautiful to forget.

Closing music: 'Never Forget' – Take That

North Kesteven District Council tributes

- I'm so sorry to hear of the loss of Julie. She was one of the kindest people that worked here and will be sorely missed – Luke Drury (customer services adviser)

- Julie was so positive about fighting this. Life can be so unfair – Christine Cooper (HR manager)
- Julie was a genuinely lovely character who has such an air of positivity and was clearly loved by lots of our colleagues – Phil Roberts (deputy chief executive)
- Julie was such a popular colleague who brought a genuine sense of happiness and positivity to work and will be very much missed – Ian Fytche (chief executive)
- Julie was a fantastic colleague to all of us and a good friend to many. She was always positive and a joy to work with. I made life difficult for her, having to learn to write 'Yorkshire' in press releases as she'd say and trying to dodge the camera, but she'd always respond with a smile and make it work. I will miss her, her love for the job and NK. Julie was a valued member of the team here and did a fantastic job for us, especially on the social media side of comms and particularly in getting out our press releases liaising with external press agencies. Julie will be missed by all – Cllr Richard Wright (council leader)
- She was so positive in herself and such a happy person. It is just so so sad – Tracy Aldrich (housing services manager)
- Julie was brilliantly ace to work with. I now forgive her for capturing me in the background of photographs (usually in the chamber or at LDW events) standing in profile ... very unflattering! Big hugs to all of you – Chris Fox (democratic services officer)
- She was more than an exemplary officer, she was such a lovely human being and it's quite impossible to believe she's gone – Cllr Ian Carrington (executive board member)

- She was such a lovely person who was so smiley and helpful, and I really enjoyed working with her – Esther Watt (corporate information manager)
- Julie was a beautiful soul and will be so missed by everyone. She absolutely loved working here, especially in the team with you guys – Jenni Swift (democratic services team leader)
- I am really sorry to hear about Julie. She was such a lovely person, kind-hearted and funny and I am really sorry for your loss – Julie Heath (senior comms officer, West Lindsey DC)
- Many staff have been sharing their sadness at the loss of such a friendly, approachable, likeable and funny friend and colleague. She turned any concern or complication into a workable solution. She was excellent at cornering unwilling participants for photographs! The staff from the Wellbeing Service all know Julie. She was a huge help during the first year of the service when we all wrote awful press releases, items for the Huddle and the housing annual report. She worked her magic and made them informative and relevant. Her consistent positive 'can do' attitude supported us all. Nothing was too much trouble for her – Fiona Jones (Wellbeing Service manager)
- Julie was such a positive person with a smile for everyone. I am going to miss her terribly. I can remember when she first joined NK and she just settled right in, it was as if she had always been here and work just isn't going to be the same without her and her pink stuff! I loved watching her grow in confidence when she discovered gym life, only Julie could be so enthusiastic about getting sweaty and knackered! For

24

such a gentle person she had an impact on my many dreary Monday mornings. I don't know what to say other than I am going to miss her – Sarah Golembiewski (emergency planning and governance manager)

- She will be so missed and was a wonderfully positive, kind and a genuinely lovely person. She was a joy to work with and I know how much she loved her job and working with you all in comms. Hard to believe that she is gone really. She will be missed by everyone that knew her – Lesley Hamilton (corporate PA)
- I hadn't known Julie for very long but her glowing positivity and ever-smiling attitude to life was truly infectious. When she shared the initial discovery of her illness and later the devastating news that it was worse than we could ever have hoped, we hugged – even though we were only recent work friends – and I felt her strength and positivity flow. She was a glowing light, an inspiration to all and a force to be reckoned with. She will be very sadly missed at NK and I would like to pass on my condolences, hoping that you can take some strength from hers and the knowledge that she now looks upon us all: happy, well, smiling, laughing and waiting for the time when she can see us all again – Emma Walkden (project officer)
- It was a pleasure to know you, Julie, what a strong and brave lady, you will be greatly missed – Michelle Towers (PA)
- I was devastated to hear the very sad news about Julie. It is heart-breaking when someone so young and full of life and joy is taken from us so quickly. Julie was one of the most friendly and genuine people I have ever known. She was always willing to help out and go the

extra mile with enthusiasm and a broad smile that always cheered me. She will be very sadly and greatly missed. I send my heartfelt wishes to all her friends and family – Jo Mason (tenant engagement officer)

- She was a pleasure to work with and will be truly missed – Emily Norton (associate editor at Stonebow Media)

Chapter 4

The Second Half

My heart was already broken when I realised that Julie would never come home.

Another huge split – one that certainly can't be fixed whatever happens next – came when I worked out that death meant that I had spent the second half of her life with her.

There was yet another blow, which was discovered during a bereavement support session. There was pain of grief not only for losing someone too soon, but also for missing out on a future together.

We met for the first time in July 1999 when Julie joined the *Northamptonshire Evening Telegraph*'s sports desk on work experience from Northampton College. At the end of her first day, I offered her a lift home in the car instead of her getting the train from Kettering.

There was a connection because she also lived in Wellingborough and supported Rushden & Diamonds FC, along with her dad. It took us only a couple of months to start a relationship, even though I was married at the time.

Our wedding day was Saturday, June 14, 2003, at Wellingborough Registry Office followed by a honeymoon in Hemsby where we enjoyed the majority of our holidays. Julie and her family love the Norfolk coast, so we were happy to spend time there.

We had wonderful trips to Cornwall, Whitby and Paris for summer breaks, plus weekends away all over the country when I was covering Diamonds' away games for the paper. We loved going to places like York, Torquay and Brighton.

We didn't want children and – although the financial situation was never anything more than fairly comfortable – we were both happy at home. Work was also going well, as Julie earned promotions with the *Herald & Post* newspapers, starting in Northampton and moving to the Bedford office.

Unfortunately, anxiety and depression took over. She took on a different role designing page templates for the editorial system in Cambridge where I also spent twenty months after taking voluntary redundancy when the *Evening Telegraph* became a weekly title in the summer of 2012.

Very briefly, we worked together on the news desk at the Cambridge News but Julie's mental health was seriously suffering from the daily stress. She made the right decision to get away from journalism and move into communications.

Julie joined the City of Lincoln Council and made the daily commute easier by staying with my dad in Boston during the week before coming home to Wellingborough at weekends. We joked that the secret of a happy marriage around that time was not being together!

Since leaving Lincolnshire in October 1996, there had been absolutely no thought about going back. However, all that changed as I re-joined the *Lincolnshire Free Press* and *Spalding Guardian* in May 2014.

We decided to sell our home in Wellingborough and move to Sleaford in October 2015 because there was already a strong indication that Julie would be offered a role at North Kesteven District Council. So it proved and we settled in.

Only three-and-a-half years later, life changed completely. Who knows what would have happened in the future, but it doesn't feel fair that we only had twenty years instead of a much longer time until retirement.

Chapter 5

Are You Okay?

How are you coping? I've been asked this question many times and honestly, I don't know the answer. Other people have given a positive reply on my behalf, which is comforting.

Of course, there are plenty of times when you feel that you can't cope. I know that I couldn't have got through those weeks and months on my own without the fantastic support of family, friends and professionals.

Probably the main lesson to learn is that there won't be a right or wrong way to deal with grief. Every person is unique and every bereavement is different.

However, there are clearly wrong things to say – some phrases and questions which shouldn't be used. People are not intentionally insensitive but at times it's perhaps better to say nothing.

There are no words that will really make a difference.

Please don't even think I'm being brave by writing this or doing anything else. I've seen true courage from Julie when she was suffering awful pain.

Don't ask 'Are you okay?' Obviously I'm not. If you ask if I'm having a good or bad day, at least there is an option to discuss those emotions.

I don't want to be told 'stay strong.' I tried my best to do that during Julie's illness because she needed my full support at the worst possible time. Since then, I think I've been allowed to feel very differently. Now I'm absolutely allowed to release my emotions and feel upset, angry or whatever else. I don't need to be positive.

'Chin up and be strong.' That was another message in early July but those words are not really helpful. This was a common theme already. The phrase is a combination of what my parents and others were repeatedly saying. Again, they are only trying to offer support. But at the first meeting with the bereavement group, I mentioned how the message is out of date. Others seemed to agree. 'Moving on' doesn't seem like it could happen, and why would it?

Another major lesson throughout this process has been the value of real friendship.

You don't have to show support every day or every week. Knowing you're available if I need you is more than enough. Thank you so much for being there.

The kindness of Julie's friends proves why she was loved by so many other wonderful people.

Until this happened, I didn't think I had many friends and maybe I didn't need anybody other than my best friend and soulmate. I was wrong and I'll admit that.

As soon as I left Basingstoke on June 21 and got home on my own, I knew that I needed support and professional help through counselling. Previously I wouldn't have asked for help, but this was totally different.

I couldn't have coped without Julie's incredible friends – and you know who you are. I hope I can offer some support as well, because I understand this is immensely tough for all of us together, particularly in the first year after a sudden, unexpected loss.

I would never even try to pretend that my emotions are worse than anyone else's. All I can possibly do is explain what it's like losing your soulmate.

Everyone will suffer grief. The reality is that we will die. But you expect to lose grandparents and parents; you don't want to think about losing a partner, particularly before her 40th birthday.

I can't begin to imagine how it feels to lose a child. However, the questions are the same in any situation – how and why did it happen?

Two words sum up the feelings since this started: exhausting and overwhelming. In less than two-and-a-half months of Julie's illness, everything was turned upside down many times.

The rollercoaster of loss sums up the feelings surrounding bereavement. Ups and downs, good and bad days (or bad and worse). The journey takes us from shock to denial then asking why me and why did it happen? There is anger, blame and sadness.

I've definitely reached 'the pit' where you feel this is too much and I want to get out of feeling like this. But then it becomes clear that you will never hit rock bottom again. There will be slight setbacks but generally it does get better through acceptance that maybe it will be okay.

I'm not at all convinced about the stage of 'moving on' because that seems such a horrible phrase. You can't forget what has happened.

I don't like my life without Julie. It's not fair. Why is the rest of the world carrying on as if everything is 'normal' when there are times when I can't cope?

In only a few weeks, I had gone through all these feelings:

I don't feel anything
I feel sick
I feel guilty/angry
I feel like crying but I can't cry
I feel exhausted
I feel I'm going mad
I feel afraid
I feel envious of other people
I feel so alone
I feel guilty that I didn't feel sad
I feel a lot better

The truth is that it's okay not to be okay. Thankfully these days, we can talk about mental health more openly than ever and we have gone beyond those stereotypical ideas that men won't talk about how they are feeling.

It definitely helps talking to those who really understand because they have suffered similar situations. Bereavement support groups and one-to-one counselling are massively helpful. I understand completely that you need some confidence to make the first step at the right time for yourself. I will share more about my experiences of bereavement support and counselling later in the book.

Personally, I found the support of friends also guided me in the direction of topics that offered invaluable strength mentally. Music, art and travel have given me an escape route and a clear head at key moments.

It would be easy to stay in bed all day. I could easily have felt sorry for myself.

There were a couple of songs that were recommended to me within a few days of getting back home and since then, I've listened to them almost every day.

'Wings of an Angel' by Lauren Alaina – on the soundtrack of a heart-warming film *Forever My Girl* – and 'You Say' by Lauren Daigle have beautiful lyrics that mean so much to me. I've also seen both of those American singers live in concert in the UK.

I've enjoyed looking at art in London, Amsterdam and Brussels to put my mind onto something extraordinary. I never thought it would become so important and I understand why it wouldn't work for other people. You need to find something that you can enjoy in 'normal' life surrounding all the grief. Don't feel guilty about it. Another big bonus has always been booking trips and having diary dates to look forward to – whether it's going to be a football match, a trip on Eurostar, stand-up comedy or a West End show. I had a peaceful weekend in the Peak District in the middle of July because I needed to get out of the house. Since then, I've appreciated all the leisure time – even though it's not the same on your own.

Chapter 6

Journal

It felt heart-breaking to find some of Julie's notebooks which she had started. One of the Macmillan support staff at Lincoln County Hospital advised her to write a journal. She wrote a couple of pages at the end of May but tragically couldn't continue when we went to Basingstoke.

Every so often life hits you with a shit stick.

I've just been whacked by a shitty branch.

Writing my thoughts and feelings in a journal has been very helpful. It started on July 1 and it's easy to fill a page every day. As a sports journalist, I suppose the journal and online blog should be something which is fairly natural to do. These are the highs and lows from the first eight months…

Monday, July 1, 2019

'Have you thought about writing a journal? Your thoughts and feelings for that day. Like you're telling someone.'

Michelle's message last night when I was struggling badly again to cope. Another good idea! The support of Julie's friends has been overwhelming really. They have always offered something to help. At times, I feel guilty sending out messages but I'm sure they want to do anything positive.

Everything has happened so quickly and that's what makes it even more difficult. Today I'm struggling to find the energy to do anything. I feel exhausted constantly and I don't know how to cope.

Wednesday, July 3

Slept overnight in our spare room, as lots of Julie's possessions had been dumped on the double bed in the main bedroom when the plumber needed access to pipes in a corner of the smaller room. At least the early start meant I could get on with the huge task of clearing all the rubbish from Julie's room. And she had only been there for a couple of months! Not even surprised by the amount of pens, handbags, make-up items and clothes – many of which still had packaging and labels. Yes, she was certainly a hoarder and obsessed with online shopping. Is it really a bargain or saving if you buy something you don't even need? Anyway, never mind, by the end of this morning I had filled rubbish bags and made donations to St Barnabas Hospice's shop in Sleaford.

Saturday, July 6

Exhausted even when it feels like I'm not really doing anything other than having a rest. When people are working long hours, I feel guilty that I'm tired constantly. All of this is mentally draining. It's not unusual to have a couple of hours in bed during the afternoon and it certainly helps.

Sunday, July 7

Another rest day, feeling tired and still not fully recovered from a slight cold.

Michelle planned to stay for an hour but we talked from 6.30-9pm. She has shown incredible support all the way through. I've had messages every day plus a few phone calls.

Are we ready for tomorrow's funeral? Probably not.

Tuesday, July 9

Exactly three months since the nightmare started when Julie collapsed at work. Never thought it would end like this.

Absolutely overwhelmed by the level of support. Until this happened, I thought I had no real friends and I didn't need anyone other than my soulmate. Julie had an amazing set of friends and so many of them are prepared to help me now. I want to help them, too. I understand it's hard for all of us to accept what happened. I'm not sure that even the funeral has brought home the reality to some people.

Incredible feeling and comforting to count up the cash and cheques in the charity box from yesterday's service. An unbelievable total of £946 was collected, so we will send £500 each to Macmillan Cancer Support and St Michael's Hospice in Basingstoke. Second session with the bereavement support group. Glad I found the energy and strength to go again.

Wednesday, July 10

Slow start today but I don't want to give up by staying in bed and feeling horrible. There is always lots to do here. Yet again I feel exhausted and I couldn't even manage small jobs like cleaning our cars. Grief is so tiring. Feel useless and I've wasted a day by doing nothing.

Thursday, July 11

Today was the first time when I haven't sent the first message of the day to anyone. I want to see which friends will continue to make contact. My sister Sarah plus Julie's close friends Vicky and Nat passed the test.

8.43pm is going to be a time on Thursday that I won't forget. Again I sent a message and got replies. It means a lot to get messages of support but I don't want to force anyone away. I know others are busy but I certainly can't cope on my own.

Monday, July 15

Good to be home. Made a few phone calls to get through more of Julie's finances but it's so tiring to deal with. When I reflect, a lot of things are getting done – but at times I still feel useless and frustrated. I want to get everything done and there is not enough energy. All of this is exhausting. Lots of messages, which really cheered me up. All the support has been fantastic – so comforting.

Wednesday, July 17

Terrible day – started off with anxiety attack (first time since June 22). Felt ill and that made me panic. Worried about a repeat of what happened in October when I collapsed in the bathroom. Julie called 999 and I had a day in A&E even though all the tests failed to produce anything more than it was probably a mini stroke. Now I'm on my own in the middle of the night. Getting messages and trying to do breathing exercises but too tired to concentrate. Rang 111 and thought they would send an ambulance. Got a call from mental health nurse who was helpful. Paramedic came but we only talked. All of this is mentally exhausting. Sent out a lot of messages to tell people what had happened and got some replies.

Thursday, July 18

Four weeks on and stuck to 8.43pm messages with friends. They all replied as they know what it means. Wonderful to support each other. No words needed – just hearts or kisses.

Much better day overall. Couldn't really have been much worse than yesterday but plenty of positives and loads of support. I'm sure everyone knows I can't do this on my own.

Friday, July 19

Another 'good' day – or at least better than many over the past month.

Saturday, July 20

One-month anniversary – so much has been done already but always more to get sorted out. Wonderful support has got me through this period. Everyone says I'm coping well but it doesn't feel like that and they don't see what happens here.

Sunday, July 21

I'm not brave. People think I am. Doing all of this is tough and overwhelming.

Monday, July 22

Hard to believe that only two weeks have gone since the funeral. Much has been done, more to do. Financial stuff starting to get sorted out. Having a welcome rest at home – not a bad day overall.

Tuesday, July 23

Week four of the bereavement support group – only three people plus three volunteers. Told them about last week's anxiety attack. Apparently it's normal. Two key phrases to come out of this morning's meeting (understanding grief and loss) – every person who grieves is unique and there is no prescribed way to grieve. Important to remember all the good moments over many years instead of the tough final months.

Thursday, August 1

Wonderful day – despite a terrible start. Awake for three hours in the middle of the night, not even sure why. So lovely to spend time with Julie's friend Nat. Looking forward to this for a while and it was even better than I thought. A beautiful friend forever.

Constantly feeling guilty and I don't want to be selfish. Tears today for the first time in a while. Generally getting better as I'm trying to get everything sorted out. It takes time, though, and I need more energy.

Thursday, August 8

Seven weeks have passed and I should remember how much progress has been made in a fairly short period. Lots of support – professional and friendship. Finances are getting sorted but all the delays are frustrating. Other plans are coming together and I'm probably ready to get back to work – much easier because I don't really need to go into the office anyway.

Monday, August 12

The start of my final full week until I get back to 'normal' by returning to the office (to be confirmed).

This was Vicky's idea several weeks ago but I'm starting a blog about Julie. It should be therapeutic and hopefully it will also help others. Part one is a fairly basic story of what happened from April 9 to June 20. I won't go into personal details but I realised that so many people – including those who went to the funeral – don't have too much information. The response shows it's a good idea. I don't want to upset anyone but the rest of the story is probably going to be more emotional.

Thursday, August 15

Eight weeks gone and it's important to reflect on what has been achieved in this toughest time. Hard to accept that the financial side takes so long because it can be stressful. Overall, though, the key issue has definitely been friendship. All the support has been amazing. So grateful.

Tuesday, August 20

Two-month anniversary – so much has happened but it feels like I'm finally making progress. Counselling and talking to friends made me realise that grief is also about the loss of time when Julie and I should have been together in the future. It's very important to think about that, particularly as it affects everyone. All her friends will feel the same.

Wednesday, August 21

Not sure what to feel about tomorrow's interment service, possibly because I don't understand what is going to happen. There hasn't been any real planning like the funeral service, so I don't know any order. No control over this. No worries, though.

Thursday, August 22

Very tough day. I didn't know what to expect but it was emotionally so hard. Almost a mini replay of the funeral but this time was a final farewell. Beautiful poem read out then Julie's casket was lowered into the ground. We placed dirt and got time to think it all over. At least there is somewhere to visit for family and friends. Main issue at the moment is grief for the lost years. Stopped on the way home to send messages at 8.43pm because I'm not prepared to stop doing that yet.

Saturday, August 24

Back to normal – relaxing morning before football this afternoon. It shows I can do this, despite all the fears over the last couple of months.

.

IN
LOVING MEMORY OF

Julie Lea

ONE AT REST

Think of me as one at rest,
For me you should not weep
I have no pain no troubled thoughts
For I am just asleep
The living thinking me that was,
Is now forever still
And life goes on without me now,
As time forever will.

If your heart is heavy now
because I've gone away
Dwell not long upon it
For none of us can stay
Those of you who liked me,
I sincerely thank you all
And those of you who loved me,
I thank you most of all.

And in my fleeting lifespan,
As time went rushing by
I found some time to hesitate,
To laugh, to love, to cry
Matters it now if time began
If time will ever cease?
I was here, I used it all,
And now I am at peace.

Monday, August 26

Proud of myself and I don't usually give praise like that. Only a couple of weeks ago, I couldn't think about going back to work for the bank holiday weekend. Yet I've done it, completing seven sports pages for tomorrow's paper. Another massive step. Lots of messages tonight on Facebook and it feels good to be back.

Lesley, one of my friends from the bereavement support group, sent this: 'It won't ever be the same but you're learning to "survive" which is sometimes all we can do! Basically, losing a partner is like losing a leg – we'll never be the same and the loss will always be there but gradually we learn to dance with a limp.'

Tuesday, August 27

After a massive week, very important to go to the bereavement support group this morning – even though I'm officially back to work full time. Reflected on the depths of last Thursday to all the positives every other day. Lots of support but also another reminder of the feeling about how other people will now consider me. I'm not just a sports editor or whatever else. Now I'm that man who went through a terrible tragedy. It's going to be hard to deal with that.

Thursday, August 29

Ten weeks gone and feeling very lonely today. Thinking about what happened at the same time tonight when we said goodbye at the hospice. I don't have anyone to touch now. All I want is a hug or holding someone's hand. Lots of messages of support from the close group of friends. If only I could just see one of them now. Probably too much time thinking it over again. Sometimes it helps but you can never switch off. You don't want to forget. Maybe I should stop sending messages at 8.43pm every Thursday but I'm not ready. Hopefully it helps others, too.

Friday, August 30

Same again – feeling lonely and depressed. Hopefully this is only a slight setback to all the progress. Enjoy staying at home and that hasn't really changed.

Coming to the end of another month – highs and lows but plenty of progress. Some frustrations financially but I'm hopeful that we are getting closer. Exhaustion of grief is finally gone and I'm ready to get more done now.

Thursday, September 5

Every Thursday is tough – will that last forever? I don't think it will be forgotten what happened that night eleven weeks ago. Maybe in the long term it won't remain this weekly anniversary when we are then dealing in months or years. The last couple of weeks have been particularly difficult, so I was determined to make sure today became a little easier. I think it worked out.

Saturday, September 7

Tough start – woke up a few times during the night. Feeling lonely again, missing hugs and touches. Just want to hold someone close.

Monday, September 9

Another terrible day. Feeling so lonely and depressed again. Midway through my third week at work but I feel like I'm getting worse. Need to talk about this at the bereavement support group. I've shared my feelings in lots of messages tonight – probably a cry for help but I appreciate all support. I need to cry but it's not coming out. I'm struggling. Always against taking pills but considering them now. It's hard to explain what is wrong but knowing a message has been received is often good enough. I'm very grateful for all support from Julie's friends. I don't like disturbing other people's lives as I'm sure they have got more important things to worry about. Also, got counselling number from HR today, so I will probably speak to them. Despite everything going on in my head today, of course I still managed to get pages done with plenty of time before the deadline. Back in the comfort zone. I'm not sure that is a good thing but I know it would be a bad idea to change anything at the moment. I don't need any more stress. Strangely weird as well that I don't like getting no post – almost like being ignored. But I don't want any more problems with financial stuff either.

Tuesday, September 10

Very long day. Feeling much better this morning thanks to all the wonderful messages of support. Another session with the bereavement support group and feeling that the next week or two could be the right time to step away. It has been so helpful but I need to make that decision soon.

Thursday, September 12

No time to rest on my day off. Went to Wellingborough cemetery with Nat. Three weeks since the interment of ashes – the plot looks lovely with so many flowers. I didn't think about personalised vases until I saw them from Julie's parents and brother. I've ordered a memorial box and vase to take next time.

Today is another anniversary – twelve weeks. It's not getting any easier and going back to work has been tougher than it seems. I can do the job but I'm tired. So much has been done and it probably looks like I'm coping well. Not 100% sure about that but I'm trying my best.

Friday, September 13

During lunch break at work, I went to print off my favourite photos of Julie and bought small frames. She is all over our home again.

Monday, September 16

Very busy day and mixed feelings. Early start to give myself an extra hour at work – even though I probably wouldn't need it. Laptop died and borrowed another one but this isn't ideal at all.

Night out at the Theatre Royal in Nottingham, I bought tickets originally over a year ago to see Gloria Estefan's life story *On Your Feet* in London on my birthday. Even a few days earlier, Julie was telling me to go there with Mum. Train tickets were booked as well. But when I found out exactly what was going to happen, I was told that I would regret going. Turned out they were right as I needed to stay with Julie in the hospice. Show was fantastic and I enjoyed it, even though we should have seen it together in June.

Tuesday, September 17

Back to normal – feeling overwhelmed and exhausted. Fed up of all this – it's too much. I know it's early days but I don't believe everything will get better. It's never going to be the same again.

The bereavement support group meeting was very helpful again, even if I'm going full circle by going back to topics which had been discussed in the first few weeks. That doesn't matter because feelings have changed in that time anyway.

Little things become more important than they should do. Feel guilty that tears won't come out but that changed this afternoon as well. Talking to Penny at work when she said something lovely about it's what Julie would have wanted. Got tissues and a wonderful hug.

Wednesday, September 18

Completed four weeks full-time at work but it's not getting any easier. Horrible day from start to finish. Nothing is going right at the moment. A few tears on the way to work. Saw an ambulance which made me think when Julie said she wished she was in there. Then I also remembered the journey from hospital to the hospice. Also cried thinking about my birthday – did Julie want to make sure we were together that day? We used to love holidays or days out on my birthday. Feeling emotional and tired today. Pretty comfortable to get work done but it doesn't feel right. Must be horrible working with me. Feel guilty to put other people through this as well. Feeling overwhelmed again like my head is going to explode. So much going on.

Thursday, September 19

13 weeks gone – very emotional and it's certainly not getting any easier to cope. People say I'm doing well but they don't know what's going on in my head. They don't see what happens at home either. Sticking to 8.43pm messages with close friends because I feel their love and support when I really need it. Need to find some energy again.

Friday, September 20

Another anniversary – three months. Woke up in the middle of the night feeling lonely again. Despite all this, determined not to feel sorry for myself staying at home with bad memories. Heartbroken.

Saturday, September 21

Lovely start, woke up after dreaming about Julie. I don't usually remember anything like that. I think we were at Dad's house but she was happy in her job. She was covering a protest – I don't know what or why. Nice to see her smile again.

Tuesday, October 1

Happy with decision to miss bereavement support group meeting, especially because I needed extra time at work anyway. It was never the major reason, though. Just worked out quite well. Feels like a positive move to step away from the group at this stage when it has been very helpful but probably gone full circle.

Thursday, October 3

Another anniversary – 15 weeks today. Six weeks of full-time work to keep me busy and much better than staying at home all day feeling sorry for myself. Lots to look forward to. I don't like to hear 'It's what Julie would have wanted,' but it's probably true.

Thursday, October 10

Six months ago yesterday, Julie went into hospital for the first time. Absolutely never thought this would happen. I understand we can't change anything now. We did everything at the time and I know she got the best treatment. It's not fair – and I remember Julie saying that many times. If this had happened to me, I'm sure there would not have been the same level of support. I wish it was the other way around. Without Julie's friends, I couldn't have coped with all this over the last sixteen weeks. I know it's okay to not be okay. I've been exhausted, overwhelmed and depressed – not all at the same time or every day but this must be the toughest experience.

Today is World Mental Health Day. I've certainly learned the importance of talking and getting support. I always gave my best for Julie, even if it wasn't quite good enough. I tried to support her through anxiety and depression. I was proud of how she battled against it. It's interesting how many people have been checking on me. Those friends on my favourites list are very special. I can never thank them enough.

Friday, October 11

Back to Wellingborough for the first time in four weeks. Went to the cemetery to take flowers. Jodie, who worked with Julie and became a very good friend, picked a beautiful arrangement with lovely messages about friendship. I took a memorial vase and ornament which were ordered as soon as I got back from Nat's visit last time. Spent just over a couple of hours with Julie's parents this afternoon. Another emotional day but it's been a good one.

Sunday, October 20

Four-month anniversary made me feel upset. Overwhelmed, exhausted and lonely.

Tuesday, October 22

Back to work and I hated it. Not just because of the first day after holiday. Fed up very quickly of listening to people talking – just get on with your bloody work! Feeling very antisocial and it would have been much better to stay at home.

Mainly got through the day by thinking back to last week. Happy memories – also a phrase that some people don't like when talking about grief. But this is very different.

Wednesday, October 23

Worst day for a long time. And it comes just when I was thinking that it may be getting better. Not allowed to be like that again, I suppose.

Woken up just after 2am with heart pounding. It felt like it was going to burst through my chest. Went on for about an hour and I spoke to 111 three times. I was just nodding off at 5am when a nurse called back and advised doctor's appointment to check heart rate.

Appointment made and decided it would be better to finish off work at home. Saw nurse this afternoon for ECG and check blood pressure. All clear, so it seems everything is stress related. Got appointment with Dr Iliffe next week to talk properly.

Thursday, October 24

Another anniversary – eighteen weeks. Soon it will become months when this figure gets much bigger. Even got frustrated in the middle of the night when I realised it was Thursday again.

Feeling much better today. Relief that there are no cardiac issues and it's no surprise that the heart palpitations are stress related.

One-to-one counselling session this morning and good to share what happened yesterday. It feels 'normal' as part of grief and trauma. Struggled to answer why I feel guilty about lots of things.

After all the problems and messages of support, it's interesting to see who checks up today. Nat got in touch and lovely to get a message from Jodie as well – true friendship.

Monday, October 28

Decided to go back to the bereavement support group tomorrow morning after missing four weeks. Feeling low last week was a setback and I want to talk about that.

Tuesday, October 29

Good decision to go back to the bereavement support group this morning, as it really helped to talk and listen. Also showed why I don't need to go every week as the topic was the same again. Emotional as it discusses the term 'soulmate', which I always used about Julie. It feels like half of me is gone.

Facebook memories showed message from Julie when we officially bought the house four years ago – although the anniversary of moving in is tomorrow. We were very happy about starting a new life. It didn't really work out as planned financially but I feel proud that we moved here because of Julie's job.

Thursday, October 31

Another week gone (19) and every Thursday is painful. Not ready to stop 8.43pm messages but I know that the weeks are turning into months. There are other anniversaries, too. It will never be the same again.

Friday, November 1

A new month and lots to look forward to. Nice to have trips booked but today was all about having a rest at home.

Grandma won't be going back home as she needs long-term care. One of those issues which make me feel guilty. I haven't been able to visit because of everything else going on. Regular updates from my Uncle Howard and Auntie Carol. Will always remember that I was visiting Grandma in Pilgrim Hospital at the time when Julie got ill.

Thursday, November 7

Feeling lonely and tired. Another week (20) and we are certainly getting to the stage where it becomes about the number of months. Realised that I might miss 8.43pm alarm and messages next week when I will be at the theatre. I don't want anyone to think I have forgotten, though.

Saturday, November 16

Starting to consider a couple of options with travelling and writing a book. Could I take time off work or have a break then do something else? It's worth thinking about. Can travel and carry on working, too.

Monday, November 18

Letter arrived to confirm that the mortgage has been repaid in full. Good to get confirmation, even though it had gone through on the app.

Not a good day at work. Very tired, early start, bored and struggling to adapt to new glasses. Pleased to get home.

Just need to get myself through the next couple of days at work then enjoy another break. Not interested in work at the moment.

Wednesday, November 20

Absolutely horrible day. Not felt like this for what seems like a long time. The five-month anniversary hit me very hard. This morning I listened to Take That's 'Never Forget' for the first time since the end of the funeral service. Maybe shouldn't have done it. Burst into tears for the first time in a while. Maybe that's also a good thing. Not happy with myself for living life on Facebook but also it's good to let people who care realise what's going on. Lots of support again. Felt terrible all day at work and just wanted to be left alone. Got the pages done but it doesn't matter to me. Can't wait to finish and have another break. Probably would have been better to stay at home as I didn't really want to speak to anyone anyway. Must be uncomfortable for others ad they don't really understand why I feel like this. Lovely message this afternoon from Julie's friend Lauren again to say how she finds it very hard. We need to support each other and I'm not feeling selfish about any of this.

Thursday, November 28

Week 23 and feeling much better after break in Brussels, plus everything else to keep myself busy. The other option is staying at home, being lonely, crying and feeling miserable all the time. It's not about 'moving on' but you have to adapt to life, even if you don't like how it has changed so much. Made another decision tonight to stop sending 8.43pm messages – interesting to see if anyone notices. It doesn't mean I will forget and the phone alarm can stay on.

Thursday, December 5

First Christmas card received and a very special message from Carol –
Thinking of you
Hope the season brings a little peace to your mind and to your heart
Remember that you are thought about at Christmas and always
Wrote cards for everyone so they will be ready to send or hand out tomorrow. Used most the packs that Julie had bought. Thought about leaving it and making a charity donation instead but I want to say thank you for all the support, too.

Friday, December 6

Feel guilty about a lot of things, some are justified and others are probably connected to grief and depression. One of the issues is not seeing Grandma for a few months while I've been dealing with Julie. Went to Grandad's grave today plus Great Grandma and

Nanny to take flowers for the first time this year. Used to visit more regularly when we lived in Wellingborough. Saw Howard, Carol and Mum at Grandma's house. Went to the care home as well. She knew me most of the time but it's very sad to see how dementia has affected her. I don't think she really understands why she is living there and Howard tried to explain about selling the house. Mum left early and it was nice to talk to Howard and Carol in the car park. Broke down a couple of times talking about Julie. Very emotional day.

Thursday, December 12

Another week gone and one more until the six-month anniversary. Lots has been done already. Alarm goes off at 8.43pm but I don't feel a strong need to send messages at this time. I'm sure Julie is not forgotten by anyone.

Monday, December 16

Devastating news that cousin Scott's son Nathan passed away yesterday. It seems to have been suicide, according to Sarah and Dad. Sent message last night to Scott offering support and knowing you can't really say anything to help. He sent a message about Julie, but this is different. There are no rules over grief.

Friday, December 20

Six months ago today, our hearts were broken. I feel so lonely without my soulmate. Thank you so much for all the amazing support. I couldn't have got through this without you.

Former *Cambridge News* colleague Raymond Brown (Facebook comment): Love can be cruel and as for death, it's a heartless thief. You just have to keep swimming.

Jodie (text): It has been a tough six months but she is still held so tightly in all our hearts. I'm so pleased you've stayed in touch and while I know it's been so hard, you are surviving, too. Julie would be so proud that you've said when you're struggling and sought help. I realise this time of year will be really hard but I keep thinking happy thoughts about her. When I look at the twinkly lights and sparkling decorations on my tree, she's often in my mind. Something about this time of year that makes you reflect. xx

Michelle (text): Been thinking about you today. Hope you're doing okay xxx

Lauren (text): You know where I am x Just remember there are lots of people who you can turn to – I'm always a message away. x

Saturday, December 21

Julie's Joggers from North Kesteven District Council raised £1,560.71 (target was £500) from Lincoln Pretty Mudder in October on the same day as Nat's Race for Life in Lincoln. Magnificent effort.

Tuesday, December 24

Final delivery of Christmas card and it's devastating as Julie's friend Gemma writes to her: 'Hope you are well.' I'll probably send a letter in the New Year to explain what happened. Obviously she hasn't been on social media and I'm truly shocked that someone didn't know.

It would be lovely to switch off my phone, emails and social media until going back to work on Boxing Day. I understand it can't be done and I wouldn't want anyone to worry at all. Just want to be left alone for a couple of days. The best way to cope for me is staying at home with my cat Poppy and watching TV. I don't suppose some people would understand but I have to make my own decision. I certainly don't want anyone telling me what to do.

Messages tonight from Nat, Carol, Michelle and Julie's close friend Clare. Very nice of them to think about me.

Julie enjoyed Christmas to spend time with family and friends but we usually had a quiet day together at home. She must have been annoyed when she asked, 'What do you want?' and I always replied 'Peace and quiet.' Nobody can give me what I want now because it would be a miracle. And I don't believe in them.

Wednesday, December 25

Message from Vicky: I hope you've managed to enjoy it. It's bloody hard after this year but we all need to do the best we can.

Messages from Nat, David and Eileen. Also from Sarah right until 1pm as I was having lunch. She said there was still time to get to Dad's – glad that I didn't go, though.

Couple of tweets on #joinin organised by comedian Sarah Millican and some nice replies, too. Brilliant idea to bring people together when they are feeling lonely. Didn't really want conversation, but nice to get involved.

Worst part of the day was cooking. Obviously no point having a roast dinner and I eat one nearly every Sunday anyway. Didn't fancy gravy, so had Lincolnshire sausages with mushrooms and potato dippers. Not quite the same as previous years.

Lots of fuss with Poppy. She knows it's different now and I'm sure that she misses Julie, too. Lovely photo shared on Twitter and Instagram.

Thursday, December 26

Finally able to tell someone about Gemma's card to Julie on Christmas Eve. Didn't want to disturb anyone else but Nat's message this morning said it wasn't a great time for her either. Agreed it's a good idea to send a note to Gemma so that is ready to be posted.

Back to work. Boxing Day football was always a highlight and it's good to get out of the house after three days. Finished at 9pm and realised that I can have next week off.

Alarm went off at 8.43pm and I didn't even realise it was Thursday again because of Christmas. Another week gone. This has been one of the toughest emotionally.

Monday, December 30

Plenty to think about and I'm sure there will be some big decisions in the New Year. Won't rush into anything and I know there are plenty of people who will offer support.

Tuesday, December 31

Don't really understand all the fuss about New Year's Eve. Just another day really and it's not going to make much difference. Also the end of a decade but it still seems to be an excuse for people to drink too much alcohol. Certainly don't see any point making resolutions – if I want to do something then I'll do it.

Wednesday, January 1, 2020

Perfect start to the year (and decade) – apart from being on my own, obviously. Train to London and memories of Julie's birthday when we went on the London Eye. She wasn't sure at first but enjoyed it. Can't remember a day as good as this for a long time.

Thursday, January 2

Very emotional day. After all the highs of yesterday, this was different and tough to take. Planned a relaxing day at home but message from Carol explaining that they are meeting again at

Grandma's house to sort out more of her belongings. Went to the care home and lovely to see Grandma looking at old photographs. Also nice when she told people that I'm her first grandchild. Long-term memory is fine, but dementia means she doesn't really understand what is going on now.

Back home to get a letter from Julie's boss, including two full pages of tributes from council colleagues. Very comforting and lots of tears reading those comments. Sent messages to Michelle and Jenni to thank them again for support. All this feels like too much so I need some help from doctor/counsellor. Struggling to cope again.

Monday, January 6

Lovely photo with Julie shared from Facebook memories and popular with friends. Will continue picking out those special memories for others to see. I don't like living on Facebook by sharing everything, but it's useful to let people know what's happening and how I'm feeling. There are lots of times when it's great to get messages of support, too.

Wednesday, January 8

Deadline day at work – first edition of *Spalding Guardian* for three weeks due to Christmas and New Year. Managed to get everything done mid-afternoon and take a break. Back home to relax and went to bed at 8.30pm. Surely tiredness is not just because of three days in the office.

'Deepest Sympathy' card arrived from Gemma after she sent Christmas card for Julie and I had to explain what had happened last summer. Relief to know that we had the correct address for her. The worst part of all this was the shock of someone not knowing what had happened six months later. The timing made it even worse as the card arrived on Christmas Eve so I didn't want to spoil any celebrations for other people by telling them. Thinking about it for a couple of days on my own made it much worse.

Thursday, January 9

First counselling session for a few weeks. It probably didn't help having that break of not talking about everything. Such a relief to catch up and on the way home I remembered a couple of things that we didn't have time to talk about. Told the counsellor, Lynn, about the Christmas card and feeling very low for a couple of weeks when I couldn't get an appointment at the doctor's either. Also told her about the letter and council tributes, which were comforting apart from the emotional timing. Not sure about spending so much time talking but there are some moments when she gives advice, too. Interesting that she explained how I had given an answer to my own questions about planning the trip to America to see Julie's school friend Becky and her family around my 46th birthday, plus what to do on Julie's birthday and the June anniversary. The most important thing is having someone to talk to and letting out all the emotion. I had tears talking about Julie's 40th birthday.

Friday, January 10

Very busy day at Grandma's house and we seemed to make plenty of progress. Broke down just before leaving when Carol showed me a gift from Julie that had been found – a small trinket box with cross-stitch flower design on the top. Lovely to know Grandma had kept it and I remember Julie making a few of those boxes. Emotional to see it again and more tears.

Monday, January 13

Horrible day, feeling miserable again. Early start watching TV and didn't fancy going to work, even though an extra hour might have made it a bit more comfortable. It felt okay until I got to the office then I really didn't want to be there or talk to anyone.

Lovely messages tonight with Nat and very supportive. I'm not going to hide anything about how I feel. She asked about the next appointment to speak with my doctor and February 20 is too far, away really. Checked again online and managed to change date to next Tuesday – much better. Plus there will be counselling at the end of next week. Also hoping to see Nat, so it should be more positive.

Just need to get through tomorrow, then I'll be able to stay at home until London on Saturday. Always need something to look forward to. I can do this.

Wednesday, January 15

Another week done at work and not easy getting through it. The last two days have been okay but I'm not sure it's what I want to do.

Thursday, January 16

Very positive day. First time on Thursday to meet friends from the bereavement support group. Even though I'm usually

66

available, I'm not keen on a coffee morning but this was a discussion group. Felt a bit guilty leaving early when they were staying for lunch but I had already made other arrangements. Lovely lunch with Michelle. She is a very good listener and I can tell her anything. Regular messages every few days so she doesn't miss out on much anyway.

Tuesday, January 21

I think we will look back on today as a massive moment and life changing. Feeling so positive that this is the right thing to do. Doctor's appointment brought forward from February . Lots has happened since the last one at the end of November but I wasn't sure where we would be going. Then she offered to give me time off to think about everything. Book another appointment for two weeks on Thursday, then I'll have another week off which was already booked due to Julie's birthday.

So many messages of support in reply. Told Dr Iliffe everything and I got the response from her that I needed. She can tell what I need to do next. I need this time to think and complete a massive decision. I can't carry on like this. The job doesn't motivate me and I can't cope.

I am not a failure if I don't succeed, only if I don't try.

Wednesday, January 22

This is probably going to become my last day in the Spalding office and also my final match report. Time for a massive change and everyone knows the decision is made already. I have achieved everything that I wanted to do in my career, but it doesn't motivate me at all now. So much going on and the doctor is absolutely right in that I need time to have a break. I don't want to let anyone down, but I have to keep looking after myself. It was tough knowing that all of today's work was probably for the last time but I'm sure that I won't miss it either. Chat with my editor Jeremy tonight and I had to be honest when he asked if I am planning to come back after my week off. He probably understands better than anyone, but I can't carry on like this. Final game – Holbeach United 1, Boston Town 0. Report, quotes and stats online before midnight and that's it – job done! I won't miss doing that when I really need to get to bed much earlier.

Wednesday, January 29

Invitations sent out for Julie's birthday meal. She would have been much better organising her own party but it's important to bring everyone together again. Also means getting lots of messages and talking to people which helps all of us.

Thursday, February 6

Time To Talk Day about mental health. Talking, listening and sharing have been so important for me over the last few months. I will always feel grateful for all the incredible support. I can't thank people enough. I've also learned a lot about family and friends.

Another week gone (33) – needed to go back and work it out because we've been dealing in months since December really.

Another emotional day. Bereavement group discussion meeting and lunch – good to talk and listen in smaller group. Understanding and support became the main topics.

Thursday, February 13

Even more emotional than expected on Julie's fortieth birthday. Many messages of love and support. Very grateful to spend almost twelve hours with my best friend Nat with lots of tears and hugs. She was a very special guest for the family meal at lunchtime with Julie's parents, David and Eileen. I had ham, egg and chips because I know that's what Julie would have wanted. Took flowers with Nat. Back home just after midnight to find card from Carol: 'Thinking of you.'

Doctor's appointment this morning and signed off for four weeks, taking me up to holiday at the end of March. It means that I can hand in my notice and serve the period while being unfit for work.

Lovely gesture at North Kesteven District Council to wear pink and get donations for Cancer Research. They also planted snowdrops in memory of colleagues.

Friday, February 14

Valentine's Day is tough when you have lost your soulmate.

Day started with counselling session and tears before we even started to talk properly. Lynn sent a lovely message for Julie's birthday and as I arrived this morning, she showed me the poster designed by Michelle to promote charity donations at the council. Too much for me emotionally and I broke down. Another good session.

Saturday, February 15

Ten close friends and I came together tonight to celebrate Julie's 40th birthday at La Rocca, Wellingborough. Lovely meal for a couple of hours and lots of happy memories. Emotional talking about the full story of what happened last summer.

Thursday, February 20

Eight months of pain and 35 weeks since my soulmate left us. Heart is broken and it won't get fixed. I know that.

This was my post on Facebook this morning: Are you okay? How are you coping? I don't know the answer. I am trying my best every day and I definitely couldn't do this without some incredible support. Thank you. I will keep talking and doing the right things. I promise.

Friday, February 28

Very emotional day. Counselling session with Lynn to reflect on resignation from work, plans for writing a book, support from friends and last night's bereavement group meeting. Broke down again towards the end of the hour when I thought about Julie's final night in hospital and the incredible care shown by the nursing staff, especially Gemma, who rearranged the beds to make sure Julie was more comfortable. Lynn talks about post-traumatic stress disorder and I need to know more about it.

Chapter 7

Poetry by Julie

These poems were found in one of her notebooks, written probably only a few weeks before this illness when she had been previously struggling at work through anxiety and obsessive compulsive disorder.

All in the Mind

What do you do when you feel like you're losing your mind
And the thoughts in your head have become so unkind?
But it's never about anyone else, you see
The only person giving me a hard time is me
One minute I'm up, the next I'm down
One minute laughing, moments later a frown
I long for the time my moods are the same
An end to what feels like a long mind game
But I have to live in the hope one day I will be free from the
misery I currently see
I wish I could find the girl I felt like in the past
Who knew sad days were ones which wouldn't last
I always used to be happy, never really sad
That's what I think makes my head so mad

Another Day

At the rising of the morning sun
Another new day has begun
The day before consigned to the past
Just memories of which some will last
Looking back will do no good
You can't change what's happened, if only we could
So open the curtains and take a deep breath in
And let the new day, and what it brings, begin

If

If I could take the thoughts out of my head
That make my day fill with dread
I would

If I could roll back the years
And take away the falling tears
I would

If I could see
What people think of me
I would

If having to be strong
Is my only option
I will

Life

Another fish in the sea
A star in the sky
I sit here and wonder as life goes by
How we all fit into the game of life
Days of happiness, joy, sorrow and strife
How do we know what the future holds?
Thing is we don't, not really, until it unfolds
Because if we did, it wouldn't be so much fun
As we'd know what would happen before it had begun
Each day we live, we must celebrate our health
Because it means so much more than wealth
So if you're feeling down and blue
Remember life wouldn't be the same if it wasn't for you

OCD and Me

One of the many differences between you and me
Is that I have OCD
It means things have to be in order so my brain
Doesn't make me feel like I'm going insane
But keeping things in order ends up not being enough
And your head gets over complicated with stuff
So now I've learnt I have to be strong
As these are just feelings which won't last long

Only words?

Think before you go to work with a cruel tongue
And consider how what you say will live on

In the thoughts of the person you've just said it to
Even if being unkind is not what you actually meant to do
Words, once they're out there and unkind,
Are not something you can go back and rewind
You may cause someone real upset
Giving negative feelings they can't forget
Would they have been so mean to you?
Well, you know the answer to that, you know you do
So before you let your mouth go to town today
Really work out if it's what you want to say

Chapter 8

Friendship

I lost my soulmate and best friend. Until then, I didn't think that I needed anyone really close to me.

Family and friends mean so much more to me now – especially those who sent heartfelt messages of love and support from day one.

It was totally unexpected to find a 'new' group of friends. They will always love Julie and now they are sharing the love with me. Of course, they were mutual friends anyway but we can still support each other and remember the good times. Talking and sharing are so important – that's probably the biggest issue that I have learned through all of this.

Inevitably, the list gets smaller as time passes. It's totally understandable because everyone must get on with their own lives. Some stay in touch every week, others less frequently.

One special person has been there every day and a very close bond soon developed between myself and Nat. From good morning to goodnight, there have been lots of messages and phone calls in between. She is absolutely amazing.

It works both ways because I'm giving something special back, too, for anyone who wants any support. I suppose that's the main reason why I'm writing this story and sharing some of the following diary entries which show a selection of the supportive messages.

Wednesday, August 28

Not a perfect time, as repeatedly thinking about this issue with how other people must consider me now. I can't control it but it's a worry. Sent messages tonight to the group of 'favourites' on my friends list with some interesting feedback.

Nat: It's not going to be easy but you are there and doing your job, hun, and doing so well, too. You are amazing. xxx

Michelle: Well done. So proud of you! Not everyone thinks of you that way so just remember that. Those that do don't really know you 😊

Jodie: It doesn't have to define you but most people will just want you to know they are thinking of you after such a tough time. Xxx

Tuesday, September 3

'He felt now that he was simply not close to her but that he did not know where he ended and she began.' – Leo Tolstoy.

Today's session with the St Barnabas bereavement support group discussed 'how to go on after your soulmate dies'. Very fitting because that is always how I described my relationship with Julie. I have a missing half now. It is said to lose a spouse is to lose the present. However, at the age of 39, we've lost the future as well. We should have spent another 40 years together. That's why I picked the topic – I feel cheated – it's not selfish but clearly it applies when you only had a 20-year relationship that ended prematurely. It was emotional this morning and I also spoke, as usual, about my feelings over the past week. Interesting to read about deciding if life is now half full or half empty. In the long term, you must adapt to your new life. There is a saying 'grief is the price we pay for love.' We also had a beautiful poem, by an unknown author, titled 'The Moment That You Died' and I had tears reading it.

Saturday, October 12

Very proud to support Nat at Lincoln's Race for Life. She had been planning to run 10k with Julie but she decided to do 5k after Vicky pulled out. Big hugs at the finish line. Tears in my eyes when the race started because Julie had done this twice for others. I could remember being there to support her.

Tuesday, November 19

Definitely feels like messages of support are slowing down. Some people don't get in touch – probably because they don't know what to say. I understand they are busy, too. Nat says sorry if we don't have many messages each day but she already does more than anyone else.

Tuesday, January 14

Nice messages from Yve, one of my close friends from the St Barnabas bereavement support group: 'Be strong and think what Julie would say. She knew you better than anyone else. If you have to leave work for a few days then do so. The main priority is YOU.'

Monday, January 20

Woken up again around 2.30am by Nat's message and we ended up chatting until 4am. Trying my best to offer support as she is understandably heartbroken about what is happening.

Nat: 'You have so much strength too to be able to give me so much support when you are suffering so much pain. xxx'

Me: 'It's a two-way friendship – we are here to support each other.'

Thursday, February 20

Nat: Thinking of you and Julie more than anything else today. Always here for you. Sending you lots of love and hugs. You too are amazing and don't you forget it. Through your pain of loss, you have also done so much to boost me and help me regain my strength and confidence again. Little steps for both of us and over time we will find happiness again xxx Thank you and I won't let you down either xxx

Chapter 9

Bereavement Support

Driving home alone from Basingstoke in June gave me plenty of time to think about what had just happened and what comes next. I knew immediately that I needed professional help.

I didn't really know what that meant. Maybe one-to-one counselling was the best plan, because I thought that would be more comfortable than group sessions. Staying at home and feeling miserable every day was not going to be a long-term option.

Talking and listening to people who understand proved to be so important. You feel 'normal' because other people have been through similar situations in losing partners or family members.

My first major step was speaking to Macmillan Cancer Support to join a bereavement support group run by St Barnabas Hospice in Sleaford for two hours every Tuesday morning.

My first session was a week before Julie's funeral. It surprised the group that I was starting so soon, but why wait if you need help now? They told me I was brave. I don't agree with that. I didn't plan to say anything at all, even though it was only a small group.

We went around the table listening to individual stories of heartache. When it finally became my turn, I changed my mind and told the volunteer that I felt ready to say something about Julie. I'm glad that I found the confidence to do it.

The first topic was 'Facing anxiety after the loss of a loved one'.

We discussed the loss of security in safety and comfort in the knowledge that things would always be okay. For some, there will be the worry of what could happen next. Are we feeling nervous or uncomfortable about the fragility of life?

One important issue coming out of this session was saying no when you're not ready to do something or go somewhere. You must focus on your physical and mental health – I learned that from the start and it became even more significant when I went back to work.

The next session was the day after the funeral and, although it would have been perfectly reasonable to stay at home, I turned up again at the group meeting because I needed to talk about it. This was exactly three months since the nightmare began when Julie collapsed at work.

The tragedy is losing Julie at the age of 39 is shown by the fact that everyone else in the support group is older than myself. I'm the next generation but I don't want anyone feeling sorry for me. Often I felt guilty adding that Julie died on my birthday, because I genuinely didn't want this to sound like a sob story.

The biggest lesson here is that there are no rules – no one else will grieve in exactly the same way as you do. There is no such thing as 'wrong' emotion. You can cry uncontrollably and, at other times, wonder why there are no tears.

My message to anyone is that talking about your grief and listening to others will help you heal. There is no time span to the whole process and no prescribed way to dealing with the intense sorrow of losing a loved one.

It became 'normal' to feel emotionally exhausted through grief. I was told that would pass in time and there was relief when those feelings finally went.

Whether you like it or not, you need to cope with changes after a loss. You certainly learn what is important in terms of friendship and support. Get your priorities right from day one. It's not selfish to look after yourself.

Daily routines are completely different, especially if you are home alone. Cooking for one, cleaning, going to work, socialising – everything in life has changed. You must adapt to this new way of life because there isn't another choice really.

One of the recommendations that I remember – even though I ended up ignoring it – was taking time over major decisions. The 'expert' suggestion is that within the first year of bereavement, you shouldn't move home or change jobs. Again, though, there are no rules.

I understand completely why in some situations people would move home. I never considered it and only a couple of people even asked me directly about it. I didn't really think that I would leave my job either, but six months later I needed to take a break and change career.

Life will never be the same again. The reality becomes particularly significant on anniversaries and other times of the year such as birthdays, holidays and family events. What seems like a minor thing can trigger sadness when we reflect on what might have been or what happened previously.

In the first couple of weeks at home, I sorted through the majority of Julie's belongings because I wanted to tidy up. I saved some things for myself, some for other people. A lot of items were thrown away, others were sold or donated to charity. I understand that this might take weeks or months for other people.

Those bereavement group sessions soon became a very important part of the week. There was some structure knowing that I could go there and share all the emotions associated with grief. It's okay not to say anything; being present and listening is taking part. Being upset is okay, too.

Even when I returned to full-time work, I continued to attend the bereavement support group for many weeks until it turned full circle by discussing topics which had already helped me during the early stages.

Stepping away felt like the right decision at the right time. As a group, we were also meeting for Sunday lunches and arranging more social events.

As well as being back in the routine of work, I had started one-to-one sessions with Julie's counsellor Lynn who supported her through a period of anxiety and depression.

There were a couple of panic attacks in the middle of the night and another incident at 2am when it felt like my heart would burst out of my chest. Those palpitations were checked out the next morning and I was given the all-clear.

More significantly in the long term, I was put in touch with Dr Amelia Iliffe, of Sleaford Medical Group, who diagnosed mild to moderate depression and offered plenty of support. We agreed that anti-depressants would be available but I didn't really want to take them anyway.

Tuesday, July 2

Today was the first major step, joining a bereavement group in Sleaford organised via Macmillan Cancer Support and St Barnabas Hospice. I arrived early, as requested, to have a one-to-one chat. I didn't think I would get involved within the group but I stayed and spoke briefly about what happened to Julie. Everyone was surprised that I had even joined the group before the funeral.

Listening to others talk about their experiences helped and it was a very useful start.

Tuesday, July 16

Week three of the bereavement support group and today I chose the topic for discussion: 'Structuring your days.' In hospital, there were no long-term plans because anything would change at any time. In the space of two weeks, we went from surgery being planned to the operation getting called off, chemotherapy ruled out, a rapid decline and 36 hours in a hospice. Since then, it has been a case of only planning maybe the next couple of days ahead. It's comforting to know I will see someone, get a job done or go somewhere. Even the small jobs are more important now as part of the day. The world has changed because of all this. There are days when I hardly have enough energy to get out of bed and I'll probably go back for a rest in the afternoon. I don't like the thought of a day when nothing is planned.

Tuesday, July 30

Couldn't contribute too much at the bereavement support group but I spoke about going back to work. They seem to think it was a big step – we'll see. Couldn't really get involved in a discussion about changing roles as that doesn't affect me particularly. Others seem to struggle cooking a meal for one or doing other jobs around the house. I can certainly manage with those because I did all that anyway.

Tuesday, August 6

Very busy start and rewarding. Usual start with week six of the bereavement support group. Dealing with stuff (literally) was the topic – sorting through a loved one's belongings. The main reason why Julie's stuff got sorted out quite quickly was tidying the spare room and wardrobe. But there seems no point keeping stuff that can't be used or donated.

After lunch, went for one-to-one counselling with Lynn who had helped Julie. Basically spent over an hour talking about what happened since the start of April but she listened and gave positive feedback. Next appointment in a couple of weeks.

Tuesday, August 13

Tough time this morning at bereavement support group. It seemed positive talking about the blog/journal idea and going back to work. Then it knocked me down in the discussion when I recalled what had happened in the hospital, hospice, back home and generally looking back over that period from April. Hurts so much to think we only had twenty years together in the second half of her life. Posted again on the blog this afternoon – comforting to get feedback. 'Exhausting and overwhelming' sums it up, so that had to be the headline. Wrote about the rollercoaster of loss – shock, denial, why me, why did it happen, anger, blame and sadness to 'the pit' where this is too much/I want to get out of feeling like this. Acceptance (maybe I will be okay) is probably my current state but this has been a bad day emotionally so I'm not sure. I know that the stages of 'moving on' and 'letting go' certainly don't seem right at all. There are so many feelings and I've gone through nearly all on the list. The world goes on around us and everyone else seems to get on with it. Life won't go back to 'normal' so eventually we need to adapt to a different way. I hope others will get help from the blog posts as well.

Tuesday, August 20

Much better session this morning with the bereavement support group. Only four of us plus three volunteers, so plenty of opportunity to talk. Didn't explain that last week's session was too emotional, but the blog has helped to release those thoughts. Interesting to see how we can adapt to life and grow around the bereavement because it's not going away or even getting smaller.

Thursday, September 5

Not the easiest start with another one-to-one counselling session reflecting mainly on the last couple of weeks – going back to work full-time, Julie's interment service and all my other emotions. Interesting when Lynn describes the brain as a computer and how I had to deal with trauma. She has picked up on several references to what happened in the hospital and hospice. Next time – at the start of October – we are going to talk properly about Julie's illness and pain. I'm reminded more recently that I'm the only person who knows exactly what was happening. I don't think Julie's messages to family and friends were always giving an accurate account, probably because she wanted to protect others.

Tuesday, September 24

Mixed feelings. I suppose highs and lows are quite normal. Not a great start as I wanted this to be my last meeting at the bereavement support group, because I've gone full circle and felt like that three times now. It's always helpful to think about issues that you don't expect to consider again but I'm ready to step away. Unfortunately, I don't have the confidence to say anything, so next week will need to become the last session. I had also taken a poem but I didn't show it to anyone. Fed up of doing things like that all the time. I suppose it's 'normal'. Exhausting. Not even enough time to have a proper conversation with anyone. Only managed brief replies to friends' messages, which would annoy me if that was the other way around.

Monday, September 30

Back to work and another busy day. Feeling guilty that everything seems okay. Better than feeling how I did. Plus I know it won't always be like this.

Decision made that I won't go to the bereavement support group meeting tomorrow. This will be the first session I've missed since coming home. I feel ready to take a break, especially this week when I've got one-to-one counselling.

Tuesday, October 8

Probably should have gone to the bereavement support group this morning, only to say thank you and explain that I won't be going back. I'll need to do that at some stage but I know I can go there anytime. I don't feel like I need to go again but there is a three-week gap between one-to-one counselling sessions as well. Feeling much better emotionally. They were right at the bereavement support group that you learn to adapt to life. This is how it's going to be now on my own and I need to look forward to breaks from work.

Thursday, October 31

Diagnosed with mild/moderate anxiety and depression after answering series of questions by Dr Iliffe. Reluctant to get anti-depressants even for short term and she agreed, unless my mood is worse when we have the next appointment. Some of the questions brought tears to my eyes when she asked about feeling down or suicidal. Glad I met her and hopefully she will be able to help.

Friday, November 15

Another one-to-one counselling session this morning. Good to talk about what has happened over the last few weeks. Some good feedback on doing the right things by working, keeping busy and having more focus on art and music to help mentally. It means much more to hear that from doctor and counsellor. When friends say 'You're doing well' it's been dismissed quite lightly, because they don't see or know everything. The most important thing at the moment is having lots to look forward to. I explained that I'm concerned over a two-week gap before Christmas but I think it will help having a rest.

Thursday, November 28

Appointment this morning with Dr Iliffe to follow up on four weeks ago after heart palpitations. Agreed that no medication is still the plan. Told her about the five-month anniversary but otherwise feeling okay most days. She seemed pleased about the trips away and asked about work. Nice to know I can see her and talk if I have a number of bad days at any stage. Reminded that everything seemed fine until the heart issues. I like what Dr Iliffe said when I was going out the door. 'Keep going' is good advice and reassuring that I'm doing the right things. Music and art have helped. Work has been quite comfortable. Having lots of things to look forward to has been very important. The two-week gap before Christmas could be a test.

Sunday, January 26

Shared messages with Nat this morning and admitted how I was feeling. Scared because some of them are morbid thoughts but I wouldn't do anything suicidal. Always honest and lovely to get support from my best friend.

Friday, January 31

Very emotional but generally a good day and I don't get many of those. Counselling session this morning was really positive – talking about all the issues at work and writing a book. She says I'm being proactive, which is good to hear. Also learned that I'm having 'morbid thoughts', which are not suicidal because I wouldn't actually do anything like that. It hurts so much having those thoughts.

Thursday, February 27

Long day but very rewarding to spend time with my best friend and show lots of support. Went to bereavement support group meeting at funeral directors in Kettering. Eight of us there with counsellor and member of staff. Quite relaxed and plenty of opportunity to talk. Feel like I can share information and I want to help others. Mainly there to support Nat, who was very emotional. Hopefully this group can become something similar to what we had in Sleaford, because that was very helpful to many of us. Nice to get back and spend more time with Nat.

Chapter 10

Back to Work

A common theme in my journalism career was about being in the comfort zone.

It can be positive because I put in a lot of hard work to get into a position where I felt I could do the job pretty easily. I had taken full control and I thought I was fairly happy.

As I've already said, I started out at the age of 19 as a trainee reporter with the *Lincolnshire Free Press* and *Spalding Guardian*. When I went back in May 2014, I had achieved my ambition of becoming sports editor.

In between, the majority of those years were spent at the *Northamptonshire Evening Telegraph* until it became a weekly title in 2012. Surprisingly to some of my colleagues, I made the decision to come out of the comfort zone for a fresh challenge.

Julie was very supportive when I took a summer break and considered a change of career. I was very close to taking up an offer to train as a driving instructor but somehow it didn't quite feel like the right thing to do.

I helped out the *Cambridge News'* weekly newspaper titles for six months then joined the daily's news desk until Julie's new career in communications took her to Lincolnshire. We were never comfortable financially but moving to Sleaford was a fresh start.

For the next five years, we worked hard just like a 'normal' couple. We enjoyed life at home as well. Then, suddenly, life changed forever when Julie became ill.

Somehow, I managed to fit in hospital visits and caring for Julie at home with getting my job done. I'm not really sure how it happened but there was plenty of support along the way.

The priority was always Julie's health and plans were in place when we went to Basingstoke. We thought that I would be able to go back to work at the start of her recovery period following major surgery because she could stay with her parents in Northamptonshire.

Everything changed very quickly and I was definitely not in the comfort zone now. I didn't even want to think about work when I was on compassionate leave, because there were much more important issues to sort out following the funeral.

I spent time with my editor's family to add to all the other support surrounding me. I remember talking to him only a couple of days after Julie's funeral and questioning whether I wanted to go back to work at all.

It took time to make the decision for a phased return by reporting on a few matches and it felt like the right moment around the start of the football season. Before going back into the office, I wasn't sure whether I was ready or not – but I needed to give it a try.

I made my message very clear in private before going back to work. I didn't want to become the centre of attention in the office. I wanted to be left alone. If I wanted to talk about Julie, I would do so – but I didn't want anyone offering sympathy when it was impossible for them to understand the overwhelming emotions of exactly what had happened here.

I needed to avoid any questions like 'Are you okay?' and I didn't know the answer anyway. There were good and bad days. Staying quiet and feeling lonely probably didn't help but there were times when it also felt right.

There was some incredible support, particularly from local football clubs, but there was always some doubt and further questions in my head about whether I really wanted to carry on doing this job.

Annual leave and trips disguised the reality of being back at work when I didn't really want to be there at all. So I made the big decision to go after almost six months.

When the doctor offered time off to think about it, we knew what I was going to do anyway. It was a breakthrough moment when I realised what I needed to do next. There wasn't a long-term plan but I simply had to get out of the comfort zone again.

Monday, July 29

Here we go again – another week. This could be a turning point as I woke up this morning feeling much more determined. Thinking about work – particularly the start of the football season – has made me realise that I might be ready to take the first step. I decided to kick off with tonight's friendly between Deeping Rangers and Peterborough United. So pleased I went. First step – maybe a small one now. It's not going to be easy but I need to be back at work, even though being in the office would be too much.

Friday, August 2

Logged onto work's editorial system, checked website and took off email forwarding and out of office, all for the first time in nearly two months. Not sure if I'm ready but I'll try my best. First league game of the season – full coverage of Peterborough Northern Star v Pinchbeck United. Job done but it didn't feel quite right. Wasn't happy being at the game as I had expected. Good to talk to the management team before and after the game, getting that first conversation out of the way helps. I know that I'm not ready for a day in the office. Hoping a few games will help to get back to work but I'm not convinced I want to do this.

Monday, August 19

Second session of one-to-one counselling with Lynn – emotional but very helpful. She asks good questions to make you think. It's going to be important to have 'plan B' on Friday if I'm not ready to be back in the office. I need to walk away and call someone for support if being there is too much. I'm sure it won't feel like this every day but at least it has been a comforting start to the week. So much going on now. Nice to be busy.

Friday, August 23

Another big step – first day in the office since April. Until recently, I felt scared over the prospect of going back to work full-time. I couldn't imagine getting past lunch when I have been exhausted every day and needed an afternoon nap. I didn't want to be the centre of attention. I didn't think I would be able to focus on the job. But those fears faded slowly. I didn't know if I would be ready but I had to try it. Counselling and friendship taught me to have plan B ready in case I couldn't cope at all. If anyone said the 'wrong' thing, it wouldn't be deliberately horrible. If someone else says nothing, that doesn't matter. Probably the big issue now was going back immediately after such a tough time at the interment service yesterday. Actually turned out to be a quiet day with no problems at all. The expectation was worse than the reality. No pressure at all. It's never going to be 'normal' but I showed that I can still do this.

Wednesday, August 28

Deadline day in the office – can't even remember when the last time was. Pretty comfortable. Needed to take a little break mid-morning but nothing serious – just cleared my head a bit.

Monday, September 2

First time in the office for Lincolnshire Free Press deadline since April and another job done – all pages sent with over an hour to spare. All about organisation and getting enough ready over the weekend. Back to normal where I could have done more yesterday but still had plenty of time today.

Change of emotion after today's deadline with back to work interview. I'm sure Jeremy thought it would be done in a few minutes. But it's not about ticking a few boxes. I don't think HR have offered any support. Even though I've got independent, professional counselling it's important that they need to put something in place for anyone else who needs help.

Big decision is that I need to book a week's holiday for Julie's 40th birthday next year. I don't think I could cope with work. How can I focus on anything? I will need a break to spend time away.

Wednesday, September 4

Two full weeks completed at work. Generally going better than expected but I've found out that the anticipation is often much worse than the reality. Quite emotional as I discussed again HR's lack of real support and it seems that I was right. At the correct time, I want some answers to find out whether they are going to help others.

Wednesday, September 11

Adrenalin got me through another day at work – so tired. It felt weird with people talking about a colleague's funeral. I'm sure they had similar conversations about Julie. At one stage I got upset and nearly cried so I went downstairs for a drink. I asked if a couple of people know what happened because it makes me feel more comfortable if I know either way. But it reminded me about what happened at a football match only a few weeks ago when someone thought Julie was recovering from the operation. I had to tell him the truth but thankfully there hasn't been anything else like that.

Wednesday, October 9

Seven weeks completed full-time at work. Before I went back, I wasn't sure if I was ready emotionally or physically. It has been very tiring but I've done the job again. The midweek matches haven't helped and I definitely need a break next week.

Monday, December 9

Final day of two-and-a-half-week break and another busy time. Not looking forward to going back to work or anything over the next few weeks. It's going to be very quiet after a busy break. Important to enjoy going out when the other option is staying at home and feeling miserable. Lots of bookings in 2020 but nothing before Christmas, so it's going to be a tough time. No interest or motivation for work but I know that I'm in the comfort zone.

Monday, January 27

Early message is that it's too soon to make a massive decision but I've explained everything. Another key moment was realising that I haven't got support at work. Although I asked to be left alone, nobody asks how I feel six months later. Presumably they think I'm coping because the job is done pretty comfortably. Mentally it's tough to be lonely with lots of negative thoughts and bad memories going around in my head every day in the office. I don't expect people to understand but I need some support, too. A good idea is working on matches as a freelance. I don't feel that I can go back on a decision to leave work. I don't owe anything to the company if I need more time off work.

Monday, February 3

Didn't even think about deadline day at work because it's got nothing to do with me now. I'm not worried about it and I'm certainly not interested in checking online stories. I've seen a few results and that's all. I always find it easy to switch off, even if I'm away for a few days. Normally I would go to football in midweek but it feels too soon for that.

Monday, February 17

Job done – resignation letter sent to Spalding this afternoon. Decision was made a few weeks ago, really for mental health reasons. I need to do this and move on. It would be easy to hold on and take more money while getting signed off work. I want to make the break and get on with it. Only back home for half an hour when Jeremy sent a message asking if I had been thinking about staying or leaving! Told him four weeks ago that I would not be coming back – certainly not going to change my decision now. It feels the right time, I've achieved what I wanted to do in my career and I know Julie would be very supportive, too.

So many messages of support over work and writing a book. Feeling positive about the future. It's not going to be easy but I can do this.

Chapter 11

The Next Chapter in Life

What happens next? Honestly, I'm not sure.

I won't be using the phrase about 'moving on' because I don't like it. Equally I can't think of a better term either.

The overwhelming pain and exhaustion from grief had gone after a few months. But there are always going to be moments of despair when you realise that life will never be the same again.

I have found acceptance of this situation in the knowledge that I must adapt to a new way of life. My broken heart won't be fixed and you can't take away the memories, good or bad.

Somehow I have to carry on by trying my best along a dual carriageway with grief alongside everyday events. Sometimes the pain catches up but you can't allow it to overtake everything else.

I'm totally convinced that, at this stage, I've made the right decision – mainly for mental health reasons – to take on the challenge of a career change. In the future, we'll find out if it works out or not.

Right now, it's all about finding happiness again. Despite the darkest times in tragedy, we are allowed to smile and enjoy ourselves.

I've discovered what really matters and I've learned a lot about myself plus others.

The next adventure was put on hold due to the coronavirus pandemic.

Ideally, the first anniversary of Julie's death – and my 46th birthday – would have been marked by a trip of a lifetime to the United States of America.

There have been a series of messages with her school friend Becky to arrange a two-week stay with her family in Pennsylvania incorporating tours of Philadelphia and New York. Unfortunately, we'll have to wait until transatlantic travel is allowed again. I'm sure the trip will happen one day and I'll find a new career, too.

Chapter 12

Inspiration and Positive Thinking

This was the title of one of Julie's small notebooks featuring some of her favourite quotes, a list of 'reasons to smile' and more thoughts about her struggles with obsessive compulsive disorder.

Quotes and sayings

'Thoughts are temporary.'

'Let the unhelpful thoughts float away; they weren't helpful anyway.'

'Thoughts are not actions.'

'It's no good putting worry onto worry.'

'Minute by minute - live in the moment. If you're okay this minute, that's what matters. You can't change the past and future isn't there yet.'

'I will do my best at all times. I think that's good enough. You'll never know unless you try.'

'I will be a good person. I don't need to be scared / afraid of things. As long as I do my best that's okay.'

'It's okay to be peed off with someone when they upset you. Burying how you feel makes it worse.'

Julie's reasons to smile

Mark
Poppy (dad)
Poppy (cat)
Mum
David
My home
My job
My health
Sunshine
Fresh air
102

Reading
Knitting
Sewing
Friends
Chocolate
Going out for dinner
Take That
Friends
The Big Bang Theory
Going for a walk
Hemsby beach
John and Sandra
Cuddles
Kisses
Laughs

Why OCD sucks...

It's only now I realise I have OCD
That's obsessive-compulsive disorder to you and me
It means many things go on in my head
It makes you live in a world of doubt
It makes you feel like you don't know yourself
It controls your thoughts
It makes you afraid
It makes you feel like you are the worst person in the world
It doesn't go away – it feeds on your thoughts and makes you
insecure
You can't tell it to shut up and go away!

Why OCD is treatable...

Thoughts are just thoughts.
Thoughts subside the less you pay attention to them.
Attention is their oxygen.
If you give in then it wins. You don't want it to win.
You've done it before, you can do it again.

Farewell My Friends

Rabindranath Tagore (1861–1941)

It was beautiful as long as it lasted.
The journey of my life.

I have no regrets whatsoever, save the pain
I'll leave behind.
Those dear hearts who love and care...

And the strings pulling at the heart and soul...
The strong arms that held me up
When my own strength let me down.

At every turning of my life
I came across good friends,
Friends who stood by me,
Even when the time raced me by.

Farewell, farewell my friends
I smile and bid you goodbye.
No, shed no tears for I need them not
All I need is your smile.
If you feel sad do think of me

For that's what I'll like
When you live in the hearts
of those you love, remember then
you never die.

Tributes From Friends

Natalie Jane

Julie Lea – my beautiful friend.

I really cannot remember a time before Julie was not part of my life and that is how much she meant to me. We met when we both worked at the Northampton Herald & Post in 2000 and we just hit it off instantly and our friendship blossomed and went from strength to strength and she was always more like family to me.

Over the years, life changed for us - the first being we both got married and then we didn't always work together. The first time of not working together was when I went on maternity leave for my first son Josh, but we never lost touch and she then became auntie Julie to Josh and later to my younger son Cameron.

She was a doting auntie and an amazing friend that was always there for an ear to bend or a shoulder to cry on. I will always be grateful that she had my back in some of my darkest periods of my life and made herself available to me on the end of the phone to chat to and laugh with me. We also had a shared love of boy bands and in particular Take That and we went to many concerts together at Wembley and Birmingham NEC to see them perform.

Even when she moved out of Northamptonshire and went to live in Lincolnshire, we still didn't lose touch and we just made every opportunity count to meet in Wellingborough or Kettering when she was back to visit family, otherwise our friend Vicky and I would arrange weekends away together. We had a very funny weekend away at Pontins for a 90s event, it wasn't the most glamorous of accommodations, it was in fact the basic of the basic, but it was the three of us together again and that was all that was important. We as usual laughed and cried together as we always had done, just like we had not had months apart. We did bingo in our onesies in the club bar and we bopped around to the wannabe Spice Girls and a few remaining members of So Solid Crew! We sipped gins and cocktails but most of all we catch up with each other's lives.

We were lucky enough to have one last girlie weekend together in March 2019 when the three of us met in Nottingham to see Bryan Adams in concert. Thank goodness we had that time away together as we could have never imagined by June that she would be taken from us so cruelly.

Nothing could have prepared us for Julie's passing and still today it is actually so hard to write the words to say that she has gone and that I will never be able to talk to her again. My beautiful friend who was always there for me through the various stages of live, who celebrated the highs and helped so much with the lows.

We were there for one another through thick and thin and I never thought we have to part as we never fell out and she always looking out for me. Forever caring and loving, like a little sister to me.

I miss her so much, hearing her voice, her laughter and seeing her amazing smile. A beautiful soul robbed of life, taken far too soon. I will never forget her.

Love always and thank you for being you Julie, just an incredible and fabulous person.

<u>Vicky Roberts</u>

Julie and I met when she started as a junior reporter on the Herald & Post. Apparently, I terrified her.

Fear overcome, the two of us soon started sharing lifts to work with Natalie, and we became a firm trio of friends; a friendship which lasted twenty years, but will continue for Nat and me, with Julie forever in our memory.

Julie was always there to listen to me banging on about whatever, and occasionally she'd get a word in to tell me what was going on in her life (usually what she'd tripped over that week.)

We had two fantastic holidays in Cyprus, where we discovered that Julie was not a good drinker. After three plastic cups of an unidentifiable cocktail, she thought it would be a good idea to get in the pool fully clothed. Turns out the security guard thought otherwise. She chuckled for around ten years afterwards.

On that holiday, with nothing else to do, we frequently played what we called the 'A to Z game,' focusing on a different subject each time, and laughing so much it hurt every time. Here's my A to Z of Julie:

A – Amazing. Need I say more?

B - Beautiful (even though she never believed it)

C - Clumsy. So bloody clumsy.

D – Designated driver. We discussed the drinking thing earlier…

E – Excellent friend. She supported me through a lot of things. I can only hope I was as good a friend to her.

F – Fun. We always had a really good laugh together. I can still hear her chuckle whenever something happens that reminds me of her, and that makes me smile.

G – Giggler. I still imaging I hear her giggling at stuff that happens or that someone says, and that makes me smile ☺ (G#2 – Gary Barlow. She'd never forgive me if I didn't mention him.)

H – Hugs. I never do them, but something made me hug her the last time I said goodbye to her, before we knew she was ill. I'm so glad I did that.

I – A word Julie rarely said. She was always much more about focusing on other people. Also, I is for injured [see C]

J – Julie. There'll never be another. She was, is, the only one like her. There will never be another one.

K – Kind. She never said a bad word about anyone (unless they really deserved it.)

L – Loving

M – My best friend

N – Newspapers. Where we met and what we both loved doing.

O – Over-thinker. Julie cared such a lot about so many things that she had a tendency to over-think things. She generally came to the conclusion that she was in the wrong, when, generally, that was the wrong conclusion.

P – Pink. We struggled and panted our way through the Milton Keynes Race for Life, both with pink wings on, and both looking pink (purple) when we finished. P is also for Pontin's, where Julie, Nat and I spent possibly the worst weekend of our lives; freezing cold, sticking to the floor, and staying in what can only be described as a cell. I had to beg Julie not to go home before Nat and I even arrived. Although it was utterly awful, the three of us had great bonding time.

Q – Questionable taste in music. 911 - what?

R – The rainbow cocktails we had in Ayia Napa. Also regurgitation – what she did with breakfast the next day...)

S – Sunburnt. She sat in the shade in Paphos, fell asleep with her arms folded and managed to get a handprint-shaped sunburn. I wish I'd taken a picture of that.

T – Tripping over. Always. Or trapping her hand or finger in something. T is also for Take That. She drove us to Aston Villa to see them and I was amazed at her confidence in forcing her way through the gridlocked roundabouts. I realise now that it was probably that nothing would have kept her from the Barlow.

U – Unsure of herself. She never believed that she was a fantastic person. I really wish that she had realised how awesome she was.

V – Vicky's best friend, missed forever

W – Warm. Everyone liked Julie because of her warm and genuine nature.

X – Erm…

Y – York, where we had a lovely couple of days away, despite walking the city walls and both suddenly becoming terrified of falling off them when we met someone coming the other way

Z – Zut alors! (Sort of an 'in joke', that one!)

Although our contact became less frequent after Julie moved to Sleaford, the minute we spoke or met up again, it was friendship as usual and giggles aplenty.

Julie, I'll miss you every day, but I'm so glad I had the chance to have such a wonderful friend for twenty years of my life. I love you loads and would actually give you a big hug if I could. Yep. Really.

Richard Howarth

An expression of life at the H&P - Julie and Vicky with my daughter Alice as a willing victim for their face painting talents in our marquee at the town show

One of the many joys of being an editor at the Herald & Post group was the chance to employ people at the start of their career and hopefully help them on the way. Julie was one of those people, joining the team in the year 2000 and becoming a central part of a special time of producing highly-regarded newspapers while having good fun in all the right places.

So many friendships sprung out of that period and you will no doubt read about them from other people but as well as being proud of giving Julie her first job in journalism – and then other more senior roles in due course – it means a great deal that we were also good friends.

During those working years we backed each other through some tough times - she was a little unnerved by some of the office banter at the outset but I helped her get through that, though she told me off for having seen past the tough exterior to see there was a big softie beneath. And, of course, she was later a key person in keeping the papers going when my daughter, Alice, was diagnosed with and then went through treatment for cancer. That period was remarkable in every way but also secured a special friendship between Alice and Julie. If Julie was always trying to keep me in check to stop me leaving too many pages to do on deadline days, Alice and Julie became something of a double act committed to giving me a hard time, in the nicest possible way – mischief was their intent, Alice now tells me. They would have their own conversations and I know they were going to be the team planning and scheming for a forthcoming big birthday of mine. And that gets to the essence of my relationship with Julie, we were a great team at work but able to build a friendship in tandem, ultimately with all my family.

Her love for her own family and husband Mark were central to her very being and she was funny, kind, had a gift to encourage and inspire all ages. But, alas, she also had this unfathomable love of the colour pink, Take That, pink stationery, Spurs and other issues we always enjoyed not agreeing on.

We stayed in touch after I left the H&P and we both went through something of a career rollercoaster. But we had so many good times to fall back on and so many good people to relate to we found our way to other chances and more good times. Alice and I have come up with our own celebration of her life, recreating the last photo of us she liked on Facebook, where we were being very childish on some swings in a village in Yorkshire. Whenever we are back there you can be sure we will be on those swings to celebrate someone who was such a great friend and who will never be forgotten x

Clare Turner

Julie, put quite simply, is the best friend a girl could have. I talk in the present because I still imagine her here - and I still talk to her. But of course she's not and that's the tragedy of it all. Ours was the most unlikely of friendships. We didn't like the same music. We didn't have much in common apart from our job but we immediately clicked and bonded, and Julie soon become my baby girl, my confidant and I hers. We shared laughter, joy and pain. We shared secrets with zero judgement. We had no filter. We could tell each other anything. We had a shared sense of right and wrong. Put simply, we had love. Just love. That's all we needed. It was a rare friendship and I felt truly blessed to know her. My heartbreak is real but I will always live in the moment to honour her legacy. Sweet dreams my baby girl.

Michelle Rose

January 2016 – the first time when Julie and I first spoke. She had been thrown into the deep end, starting a new position, a colleague who permanently worked at home – and at this very point in hospital caring for her son, and a whole new world in local government. We first spoke over the phone, where I tried to give as much advice and guidance as I could during this crazy time, and it was from this point that a friendship blossomed. Julie didn't know me, but instantly cared about my situation and how she could help take any burden off of me rather than the other way around. We were equal – and, supportive of each other. Julie wasn't the most confident in herself to start with, but over time that confidence grew and she grew with it. She would always say to me 'I wish I was more confident like you', and my response would always be 'If we were all the same, the world would be very boring. Instead it has got us two crazy fools – just the way we are now and I am happy with that!'

It was so lovely to see her come out her shell more over the years, approaching people at events we ran, taking up new hobbies and making new friends – in place she had never lived or worked before

I could speak to Julie about anything and she would always be there to listen, she supported me in work and out – we shared our frustrations, and our happiness.

We always joked when I was in the office with the team that we should have a Channel 4 'Office Style' sitcom. We had such a laugh we wanted the world to see, or at the very least the UK!

We would speak almost every day about something or other. We just got each other!

I try not to think about the period she took ill, I like to remember the good times; the fun and laughter we shared, the cheese and bacon scones we loved, her thoughtful nature and her kind heart.

She may be gone, but she won't be forgotten. Love you Julie Lea!

Lauren Archell

Julie was the kind of friend that you have once in a lifetime. The kind to send you a text out of the blue just to see how you were and let her know she was thinking of you, the kind who listened without judgement, the kind you'd ring first if you needed some advice. I was incredibly lucky to meet Jules in my first 'proper' job. She scooped me up, took me under her wing, protected me, advised me, reassured me, and fed me ham, egg & chips from 'Spoons and a mint hot chocolate from Costa on a Friday lunchtime with a good old natter. We both left that job, but by that time we were more than colleagues, we were friends – really, really good ones. I can't quite explain how much I miss her, but am so thankful to have had someone in my life to show me what true, long-lasting, there through anything friendship is – every day I try to be 'a little bit more Jules', and I know that would make her smile.

Ian Gallagher

It still feels strange writing this in the past tense, but Julie was everything you would want from a friend. Caring, thoughtful, compassionate, non-judgemental and selfless to the last. When Julie was ill, my mind played an unfortunate trick on me. When I felt like I wanted to speak to someone about what was happening, one of my first thoughts was 'I know, I'll text Julie.' She'd have been the first person to support me if this was happening to anyone else in my life, and it was particularly cruel that someone who was always so concerned about the welfare of others was in this position. Despite the awful situation she faced, Julie never complained to me once. She was anxious, of course – who wouldn't be? But she was always positive, always talking about the future and how she could get better. In our fifteen years as friends, we supported each other through some of our toughest times and made many happy memories when the going was good. And I think that's the mark of true friendship. I miss Julie enormously, and I always will do.